G000069139

County Maps and Histories Series
Sussex

Valerie G. Scott
and
Hugh Barty-King

Quiller Press

Published in Association with
ST. JOHN SMITH

This highly decorative title cartouche appears on a map by Richard Budgen published in 1724, which was the first large-scale map of Sussex. It contained a great deal of information which had not previously been published like the location of iron furnaces and forges, a theme taken up on the left of the cartouche. This was also the first map to be oriented to true north and to indicate magnetic variation.

Little is known about the life of Budgen, except that it was short (1696–1731), or his career, except that he also prepared some estate plans and wrote a pamphlet called The Passage of the Hurricane from the Sea-side at Bexhill in Sussex to Newingden-level. The twentieth of May 1729, which was accompanied by a plan. (By courtesy of The British Library)

Quiller Press Ltd., 50 Albemarle Street,
London W1X 4BD.

First Published 1985

ISBN 0907621 56 2

Designed by Tina Dutton
Design and production in association
with Book Production Consultants, Cambridge
Printed by The Burlington Press, Foxton, Herts.

The county maps and history of

Sussex

Valerie G. Scott and Hugh Barty-King

The distinctive character and history of the county of Sussex derives from a fertile soil and warm climate, from the Andresleage or Andredesweald, the dense forest which once covered half of it, but above all, from the seventy-five miles of sea coast lying within fifty miles of the European continent. When, in 1585, William Camden wrote of the Sussex of four hundred years ago in his *Britannia*, he confined himself to surveying the coast. 'The inner parts of the county being thick set with villages have nothing very remarkable.'

The sea gave the people of Sussex fish to eat and sell; when rough it threw ships on the rocks for them to plunder; it provided an honest living for shippers and shipbuilders, and a dishonest one for smugglers and pirates; it was the channel which carried peace-loving refugees to and from Britain; it was the watery frontier to be passed by would-be conquerors seeking the foothold which would lead to the subjection of the island and its inhabitants.

Notwithstanding the intentions of those who rode on it, good or bad, the sea itself was an enemy. For century after century the people of Sussex could do little to prevent it from changing the shape of its coastline. The movement of shingle from west to east clogged up the mouths of the rivers slackening their pace and forcing them to deposit silt in their estuaries instead of the sea. Shoreham had been a busy port in the thirteenth century, but by 1585, as Camden explains, it had been 'destroyed and swallowed up by the sea, and the harbour has lost all its convenience by the sands driven up to the mouth of the river, whereas in former ages ships used to come up under sail to Brembre [Bramber] which is farther from the sea.' Winchelsea was England's greatest exporter of timber in the Middle Ages but by Elizabeth's time the harbour had become completely silted up. A big storm had overwhelmed it in 1252 'at which time,' wrote Camden, 'a great alteration was made in this coast and the neighbouring coast of Kent.' A knock-out blow from a tempestuous sea in 1287 delivered the *coup-de-grâce*. The sea lapped the east and west walls of Pevensey Castle up to 1700, and was still eroding the fragile coast line of Sussex when Daniel Defoe travelled through the county on horseback during his *Tour Through the Whole Island of Great Britain* in 1724. The sea was very unkind, he wrote, to the fishing village of Bright Helmston, which was not to become the famous watering place Brighton for another fifty years.

> The sea has by its continual encroachments so gained upon them that, in a little time more, they might reasonably expect it would eat up the whole town, above 100 houses having been devoured by the water in a few years past.

Early Days

A storm drowned some forty men of the five legions and 2000 cavalry whom Julius Caesar brought with him in 800 ships for the second landing he made at Sandwich in 54BC after the three week reconnaissance raid of the year before. He advanced a hundred miles and then withdrew to Gaul without ever entering what is now Sussex. The county was also by-passed by Plautius whose landing with a more formidable army at Sandwich some ninety years later and subsequent defeat of the combined 'British' army under Caractacus, signalled the start of the Roman Occupation. After their victory, the army of Plautius, soon joined by another led by no less a commander than the Emperor (Claudius), marched northwards to Colchester. But had they turned south to subdue the Regni, they could have availed themselves of one of the seven roads of Ancient Britain, Ermyn Street which joined Sussex to the South East of Scotland. One branch of this road began in Pevensey and ran through Eastbourne, Mayfield, Wadhurst, Tunbridge Wells and Bromley; another began in Chichester and ran through Pulborough, Stone Street, Coldharbour and Dorking. The two branches met in London at Ermyn Street and from there ran as a single road to Scotland.

Between 420 and 440 the sea bore Britain's sophisticated Roman occupiers away, having given their remote colony a taste of civilisation which in the Dark Ages ahead became only a faint memory. Their most solid monuments, part of which stand today, are the fort they built at Pevensey (Anderida) and the remains of the town they called Regnum (Chichester) where there was a temple dedicated to Neptune and Minerva by King Tiberius Claudius Cogidubnus, Imperial Legate in Britain. There was a concentration of villas around Venta Belgarum (Winchester) with a strip running past Chichester to the neigbourhood of Brighton. In 1961 archaeologists discovered at Fishbourne (Noviomagus Regnensium), at the head of a sea creek one mile west of Chichester, the remains of a palatial Roman villa occupying some five and a half acres. From its early date (around 75 AD), its enormous size and its elaborate winged corridor plan, it was an exceptional find. 'It is the sole villa in Britain,' said Sir Ian Richmond, 'which can be recognised immediately as an imported Italian type.' It had remarkable black and white mosaics and a striking head of Medusa. It seems to have been occupied well into the third century and was likely to have been demolished following a fire in the year 270. Twelve miles to the east of it Roman pavements were uncovered at Angmering; in the courtyard villa found at Bignor the decoration included cupids dressed as gladiators. The dense Anderida Forest kept them from settling in any other part of Sussex.

In 477 the sea carried three ships to Sussex bearing the advance party of barbarians who were to give the county its name, the South Saxons. Ella and his three sons put into the harbour which he re-named Cissanceaster after his son Cissa. They were not the first warriors to be attracted by the fertile soil and warm climate of southern Britain; in 499 the German adventurer Hengist had established the Kingdom of Kent next door to Sussex. It took Ella the South Saxon thirty-two years after his landing at Chichester to found the Kingdom of the South Saxons covering the whole of the domain of the Regni (Surrey and Sussex). The turning point was his seizure of Anderida (Pevensey) in 490.

Three different continental nations – the Saxons, the Angles and the Jutes – descended on southern Britain in the wake of Hengist between 450 and 590 and, with the absence of the Roman legions, easily subdued the local populace whose lifestyle of the last 350 years had been peaceful and industrious. Such Romano-Britons as remained in Sussex were reduced to servitude and forced to cultivate, for the benefit of their new masters, the land which had so recently been their own. The boundaries of 'Sussex' were ever-changing. In 607 it was absorbed into the Kingdom of the West Saxons (Wessex); in 661 it became independent under Ethelwold King of Sussex. But nothing could shift the thick Andredesweald and the marshes around Rye which for centuries insulated it from the rest of Britain. Though Pope Gregory sent the monk Augustine to coax the fierce English away from the Celtic form of Christian worship to the Roman version in 597, the South Saxons were not converted until 681. The forest saved Sussex from occupation by the Northmen (the Danes) between 835 and 878, but by then the county had become part of the 'England' over which the great Alfred claimed to be sole ruler. Sussex was an important part of that kingdom, and when Alfred's grandson Athelstan became King of the English in 925, there were two royal mints at Lewes and another at Hastings.

But trees, however closely packed, were no defence against the determination of a warrior like William the Bastard, Duke of Normandy, whose English cousin King Edward the Confessor had bequeathed him the throne of England in his will. He was not the only claimant, however, and he knew that when Edward died he would have to make good his claim by force of arms. Two local men contested his right to the succession, Harold and Tostig, the sons of the great military commander Earl Godwin, one-time Sussex herdsman who now owned forty-four manors in Sussex and was overlord of Wessex, Sussex, Kent and Essex. Harold had the advantage of being the man on the spot but by a strange mischance, two years before the old king died, he was forced to acknowledge William's claim. One evening in 1064 he set out on a sailing trip from Bosham in Chichester Harbour, where forty-four years before King Canute had built the church of the Holy Trinity on the stones of a Roman basilica. A storm drove him on to the coast of Normandy at Ponthieu. When the news reached Duke William at Rouen he 'invited' Harold to pay him a visit. While a 'guest' in his castle, Harold was made to swear an oath on a casket of holy relics that he recognised his host (or gaoler?) as Edward's successor. He was then allowed to return home unharmed.

Sussex (combined with Kent, Surrey and Middlesex) by Christopher Saxton, 1579

This map comes from a copy of Saxton's famous atlas of England and Wales which is believed to have belonged to James I. Although it is a combined map showing other counties in addition to Sussex it is extremely important in the history of mapping as it gives an amazing amount of accurate detail of towns, rivers and geographical features.

Christopher Saxton is known as the 'father of cartography' because he made the first survey of England and Wales. It took him eight years, starting in 1570, and when you take into account the difficulties he must have had to overcome with the appalling state of the roads in those days and the danger of highwaymen, it is an amazing feat and one which was not to be repeated until the nineteenth century. His maps were copied time and time again by other mapmakers.

Saxton, who worked under the patronage of Thomas Seckford, Master of Requests to Elizabeth I, names 280 familiar towns and villages in Sussex and ten houses. Only two remain unidentified – Bisshops Wood near Hailsham and Woking near Lewes. He exaggerated some of the coastal features particularly the bay between Feringe and New Shoreham but all the other features are basically correct. The Flemish engraver of the map was Remigius Hogenberg. (By courtesy of the British Library)

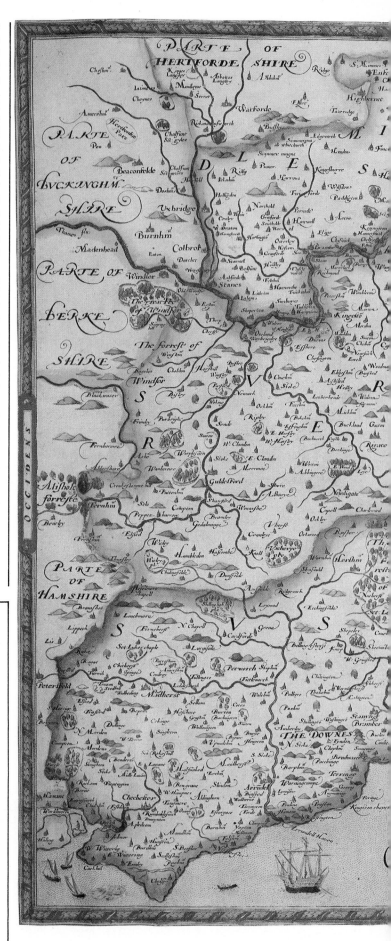

PAR TE OF
ES SEX

KENT

SEX

THE DOWNES

OCEANVS

ORIENS

CANTII, Southsexiæ, Surriæ, et Middelsexiæ comitat. Una cum suis Undique confinibus, Oppidis, pagis, Villis, et fluminibus, in eisdem, vera descriptio.

Scala Milliarum

PESTIS PATRIÆ PIGRECIES

Cantium

Southsexia

Suria

Middelsexia

Londinum

Christophorus Saxton descripsit

When the Confessor died on 6 January 1066 the Norman duke across the Channel immediately declared himself King of England, and when the English Council of Ministers, the Witanegemot, gave Harold the crown, William denounced him as a usurper. William prepared for the invasion of 'his' kingdom by infiltrating the Sussex harbours of Hastings, Rye and Winchelsea. He already had a Fifth Column in the inland harbour of Steyning which was run by the Norman abbey of Fécamp. In May 1066 William persuaded Harold's brother Tostig, who resented being passed over by the Witanegemot, to ravage the coasts of Sussex, Kent and the Isle of Wight, as a softening-up exercise. Harold organised a force to defend the coast from the attacks of his treacherous brother but when, on 6 September they were called off, he disbanded it. In the meantime William was assembling his invasion task force of 900 ships and 60,000 soldiers, mostly cavalry, on the Normandy shore at St Pierre-sur-Dive.

Tostig's Sussex raids ceased because he had set off by sea to the north-east coast where he landed his army and marched it, after linking up with the troops which landed a few days later under Harold Hardrada of Norway, on York. King Harold was still watching the English Channel for sign of William's fleet, and when he heard of his brother's re-appearance he led his army north to face the insurgents head on. He refused Tostig's offer to call off the fight and share the kingdom. On 25 September at the Battle of Stamford Bridge he put paid to his brother's ambitions of royalty by annihilating his army and leaving him, along with his Norwegian ally, dead on the field.

On the other side of the English Channel, William took the opportunity provided by his rival's preoccupation with the family dispute up north, and within four days of Harold's victory in Yorkshire, risking a storm but emboldened by papal blessing, he set sail for the Sussex coast. At the head of the great Norman army of conquest, his ship the *Mora*, landed him at Pevensey Bay unopposed. As he leapt on shore the Bastard stumbled. Recovering himself, the story goes that he grabbed a clod of Sussex earth and cried (in French, of course), 'By the splendour of God I have taken seize of my kingdom! The earth of England is in my two hands!'

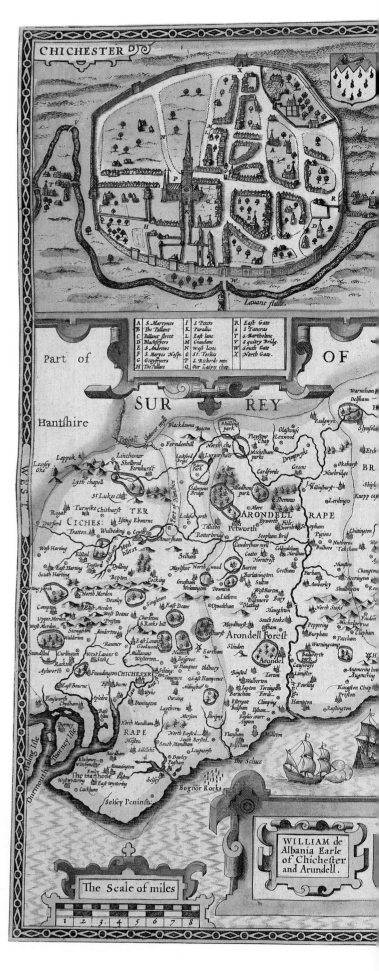

Sussex by John Speed 1610

John Speed (1552–1629) is undoubtedly the best known of all the English mapmakers. His 'Sussex Described', based on an earlier map by John Norden, appeared in his most famous work, The Theatre of the Empire of Great Britaine. *Sussex was the only county which was divided into six 'rapes' (Speed was one of the first mapmakers to show them) which were said to have been created by William I for the purpose of defence. The main difference between Norden's map and Speed's is the spelling of some of the place names. Speed also placed an island off the coast near Hastings, an error which persisted until 1723. He obviously did not feel it was necessary to show any roads. The inset at the top right shows Chichester and at the bottom the arms of four Earls of Sussex. The map was engraved by Jodocus Hondius in Amsterdam and printed in London.*

Speed was born at Farndon, Cheshire, and was a tailor by trade but his great passion was for history. He was supported in his atlas and history projects (he also produced a History of Great Britaine*) by Sir Fulke Greville who obtained permission from Queen Elizabeth I for him to work at the Custom House in London. His maps are very attractive but are definitely based on the work of other mapmakers rather than on an original survey. Speed admitted this in his well known statement, 'I have put my sickle into other men's corn,' but this should not detract from the great contribution he made to cartography, his maps still being issued nearly 200 years after his death. (By courtesy of the British Library)*

SUSSEX Described and divided into Rapes with the situation of Chichester the cheife citie thereof. And the armes of such Nobles as have bene dignified with the title of Earles since the conquest and other accidents therein observed.

Described by IOHN NORDEN. Augmented by Iohn Speede And are to be sold in popes head Alley against the Exchange by I.s. and George Humble cum privilegio.

PART

RT

PART OF KENT.

DIEV ET MON DROIT

Oxney Island

PEVENSEY RAPE

HASTINGS RAPE

LEWES RAPE

Pevensey Mershe

THE BRITISH SEA

IOHN FITZ Allan Earle of Sussex et Arundell.

PHILLIP Howard Earle of Arundell.

ROBERT Radcliffe Earle of Sussex

WILLIAM the Bastard, Duke of Normandy, making his Clayme to the Crowne of England, by affinitye, adoption and promisse, arrived at a port in Sussex called Pensey with 896 shipps furnished for warr the 28 of September, y yere of Chrifts incarnation 1066. And the 14 of October following beyng Sattordaye, nere Haftings in y same Coutie ioyned battayll with Harold King of England, whoe in y feilde valliantly fighting was there slaine by the shott of an arrow into his braynes: and with him dyed Gerth and Leofwine his brethren, and 67974 men besydes. The place where they fought, ever since doth in memory thereof beare the name of Battayll, where the Heptarchie of the Saxons was Brought to y last period. Having all their lawes altered, their Nobles displaced, and all men disherited: all seased into the Normands hande, whoe made him selfe Lorde of all, and on y daye of Chr. his natiuitye in y same, yere was crowned at Westminster King of Englande, which he gouerned the space of 20 yeres, 8 moun thes, and 16 dayes.

Iodocus Hondius caelavit Anno Domini 1610.

A portrait of John Speed (1552–1629), the well known historian and mapmaker whose map of Sussex appeared in the atlas The Theatre of the Empire of Great Britaine *published in 1611. (By courtesy of the British Library)*

Harold had no choice but to rally his victorious but exhausted soldiers and trudge back to Sussex. It took him sixteen days. Once down south again he set about re-forming his army, mostly foot soldiers, and enlarging it. His spies told him of the great size of the Norman force which had now consolidated and was moving on horseback out of Pevensey in the direction of Hastings.

Finding recruits from the men of Sussex for the Anglo-Saxon army which was to save them and their fellow Englishmen from foreign domination was not easy. Most of them, who were not fishermen, were farmers and it was harvest time. Turning points in history are rarely recognised as such by those who live through them. For the people, 1066 was just another year; Harold's call to arms just another interference with the essential business of reaping. By 14 October Harold had mustered all he could hope for, and drew them up to face the Norman would-be conquerors on a hilly landscape some five miles north of Hastings. And there, as William Camden reported some 500 years later, 'the fate of England was determined and the Anglo-Saxon empire brought to an end.'

The English put up a spirited resistance. The fighting continued fiercely throughout the day, with the mounted invaders getting the upper hand and then the battle axes of Harold's infantry cutting through the Norman armour and routing the enemy in seeming retreat. But when King Harold was killed by a chance arrow which pierced his eye, the Anglo-Saxons lost heart and fled. A large number of Harold's army, mostly from Sussex, lay dead.

Thus Sussex was the scene of the most momentous event in our history, the start of a permanent change in culture and lifestyle for all its inhabitants, more thorough and enduring than Romanisation, with Norman nobles becoming the new ruling class and French the language of law and government. It rescued England from the fragmentation of the Dark Ages and welded the tribes into a single nation, but for those who lived through the process it was a humiliating and crushing experience. The survivors of that terrible day in October 1066, who had helped Harold defend his heritage, paid for their loyalty by having their houses confiscated and a feudal system imposed on them by which they held their land in return for military and other services to their lord. The men of Kent, on the other hand, who refused to come to Harold's aid, were allowed by the Norman occupiers to retain their legal system of Gavelkind by which there was no obligation to do military service. The whole family inherited in Kent, not just the eldest son who became rich while his brethren remained poor. As William Horsfield, the great Sussex historian, said in 1835

> The cultivators of the soil of Sussex in those days were rendered in fact the absolute property of the Lord of the Manor who sold, exchanged and punished them at his will or pleasure.

For generations after the Norman Conquest, Sussex farms were held by vassals in consideration of furnishing personal, military and other services to the baron. No one could inherit a property from his father; the lord could not have a child or a woman holding land on conditions they could not perform. He appointed an able-bodied soldier to take over the farm. The rustics, or boors, of Sussex belonged to their lords as much as those of Russia at the time Horsfield was writing. An eleventh century Sussex baron referred to his 'next boor' – neighbour!

To commemorate his victory King William the First of England founded a monastery dedicated to St Martin which he ordered to be built on the field of battle, with the altar of the church on the spot where Harold fell. It was called La Batailge or, up to 1316, De Bello, and was not ready for consecration until seven years after William's death in 1094 when the ceremony was performed by his son King Rufus. Under its royal charter, Battle Abbey was declared a sanctuary in which no robber or murderer who fled to it could be molested and must be allowed to escape. A more important privilege, however, was its freedom from episcopal jurisdiction. Houses were built around the monastery which became the town of Battle.

William at first refused to hand over the body of the slain Harold but finally agreed to sell it to the dead king's mother for £6 13s 4d, and she had it buried not in Sussex but at Waltham Abbey. The Anglo-Saxon aristocracy counted for little in the land of the new regime, and the French king made his relations lords of the six vertical areas into which he divided Sussex and called Rapes. Each had a castle, from which it got its name, a harbour, a river and a road towards London – and no other county in England was divided in this way. They were the Rapes of Chichester, Arundel, Bramber, Lewes, Pevensey and Hastings – and some historians contend that they were ancient Saxon provinces which the Conqueror found and converted into feudal castelries. However that may be, William began by giving the whole of Sussex west of the River Adur to Earl Roger of Montgomery as the Rape of Arundel, along with eighty-three manors. The Rapes set a social pattern on Sussex until the eighteenth century. The new king gave the manors of those he had defeated to the men who had helped him win the one-day battle of 1066, including the manors of Bosham and Reredfelle which had once belonged to Earl Godwin. He gave the most – 108, mostly in the Rape of Hastings – to William, son of Robert Earl of Eu, his cousin and favourite army commander. To his half brother Robert Earl of Moreton, whom he made Earl of Cornwall, he gave eighty-one manors in Sussex, and 712 in other counties. He gave another near relation, William de Warren, the borough of Lewes and forty-three Sussex manors. Altogether some 350 manors were taken from their owners and handed over to Norman nobles.

The word 'rape', unique to Sussex, derived from Old English 'rap' (rope) meaning the fencing off of property by a rope and then the land so divided. It first appeared in the Domesday Survey which William ordered to be carried out between 1081 and 1086 to make sure he was getting the most out of Danegeld, the annual tax on every hide of arable land which, to the fury of Sussex farmers, was raised from two to six shillings in 1086. The

survey showed that at the lower level of administration Sussex was divided into sixty-three 'Hundreds' which remained well into the nineteenth century.

There were few monastic establishments in Sussex at the time of the Conquest and few parish churches. But the famous Archbishop Dunstan had built a wooden church at Mayfield with incorrect orientation to the east which, it is said, he righted by giving one of its sides a shove with his shoulder. It was at Mayfield that Saint Dunstan, as he became, was said to have had a confrontation with the Devil, and had the presence of mind to seize him by the nose with a pair of tongs. In the ninth century Sussex had a holy man of its own in Saint Cuthman.

The Norman Occupation saw an upsurge in ecclesiastical building with William de Warenne setting the pace in following his leader's foundation of the abbey at Battle with the establishment of a priory at Lewes. A large number of other Norman nobles founded monasteries, often connected with a French house and mostly Benedictine, in their new domain to repay the deity for victory and ensure a place in heaven for their souls by regular masses. But other orders came too – Cluniac and Franciscan monks at Lewes, Cistercians at Robertsbridge, Premonstratensians at Bayham and Otham, Austin Canons and Friars at Hastings and Rye, Carmelites at Shoreham. They were self-supporting with vineyards, wineries and fish farms, and in the privacy of their mostly closed orders they became cut off from the laity, a race apart in the England of the Middle Ages when Christianity reached its lowest ebb.

Fishing not fighting

There was no shortage of fish to be caught in the sea by those who lived on its edge, and entries in the Domesday Book show that many Sussex manors paid heavy rents in herrings. Before 1066 Hastings's boats met those from Yarmouth on the fishing grounds off the east coast in friendly co-operation, though later they fought each other in savage rivalry. But the King would have preferred them to reserve their energies for fighting the King's enemies, rather than themselves, as sailors in the King's Navy. The French were fast getting command of the English Channel, and in 1339 landed fifteen galleys at Eastbourne. But there was little hope he would get much response if the emergency came in August when the mackerel season made fishing and not fighting the priority. Hastings was the chief of the so-called Cinque Ports. It was required to supply twenty-one ships in war time, each manned by twenty-one stout, well experienced, well armed men, in return for considerable privileges. Winchelsea and Rye, the other two in Sussex, only had to contribute two ships each. The ports had to be given forty days notice, and the craft would then be on call for fifteen days at their own expense. If they were needed longer, the King paid them. By the beginning of the thirteenth century King John had a fleet of fifty-one galleys of which two were laid up at Rye where there was a shipbuilding yard, and two at Winchelsea, both of which had now become more important than Hastings.

Each of the Cinque Ports had its Admiralty Court to ensure a proper sharing of the spoil from ships wrecked on Sussex rocks. In 1263 the Earl of Warenne had the right to despoil all wrecks off the Sussex coast to the westward, and as far east as a man standing on the Whasbetel Rock at Seaford could throw a hatchet with his right hand while holding his hair behind his right ear with his left hand. While throwing the hatchet the man could not raise his right arm above his left.

The decision to wage war and raise taxes was the King's alone, and though the barons had wrung many promises of good behaviour from King John at Runnymede in 1215, a section of them sought to end the arbitrary rule of a dictator responsible only to himself. Sussex became the scene of an event even more important than the signing of the Magna Carta, the battle in 1264 in which the barons led by Simon de Montfort, Earl of Leicester, beat the army of the impecunious Henry III at Lewes. For, with the king at his mercy, Simon extracted his signature to the historical document known as the Mise of Lewes. This gave England its first Parliament – a body of men to advise the king on how he should act in the best interests of his people. It consisted not only of twenty-three barons and 120 churchmen, but several Knights of the Shire from the counties, and burgesses from the towns. The Parliamentary form of government which Britain still enjoys 700 years later stems from that heady engagement around Lewes Castle.

Sussex by Joan (John) Blaeu c. 1645

At the beginning of the seventeenth century, Amsterdam was becoming very important for trade, partly because it was the centre of the banking and diamond industry and partly because it was the base for the powerful Dutch East India Company. It was in this climate that the Blaeu publishing house was founded by Willem Janszoon Blaeu in 1599. The firm flourished and produced a wealth of maps, globes, sea charts and topographical works. After the death of Willem in 1638 the business was carried on successfully by his two sons, Joan and Cornelis, who also started to publish atlases. Joan carried on alone after Cornelis had died and became cartographer to the East India Company and a Councillor of the city. Sadly, his luck changed in 1673 when one of the printing presses and much of the stock of the company were destroyed by fire and he lost his place on the Council. Within a year he was dead. His son, also Joan, sold the remaining engraved plates to other publishers for re-use and the demise of the great firm of Blaeu was then complete.

This map, 'Suthsexia', was published by the first Joan Blaeu and appeared in the atlas Theatrum Orbis Terrarum. *Like all their other county maps, it is based on the work of John Speed but with many changes and additions. However, the Blaeu maps are remarkable for their high standard of workmanship. They used the best paper, the best workmen, the best colourists of the day (many of the maps were heightened in gold) and Sussex is a good example of the beauty of their work. Even the fleet of ships off the coast are engraved in the minutest detail and the whole map is clear and easy to read. Roads have not yet appeared but the rivers, towns, woodlands (even the windmills) are shown and, as with the Speed map, the county is divided into 'rapes'.*

It is interesting to see that Blaeu has marked 'Old Winchelsea Drowned' (right of the picture) referring to the old town of that name which was gradually washed away by erosion and finally vanished under the waves in a violent storm of about 1250. Edward I ordered the rebuilding of the town on a site further inland and work finally began about 1292. The design and plan were based on French new towns of the period and this influence can still be seen today. (By courtesy of Cartographia, Southampton Street, London WC2)

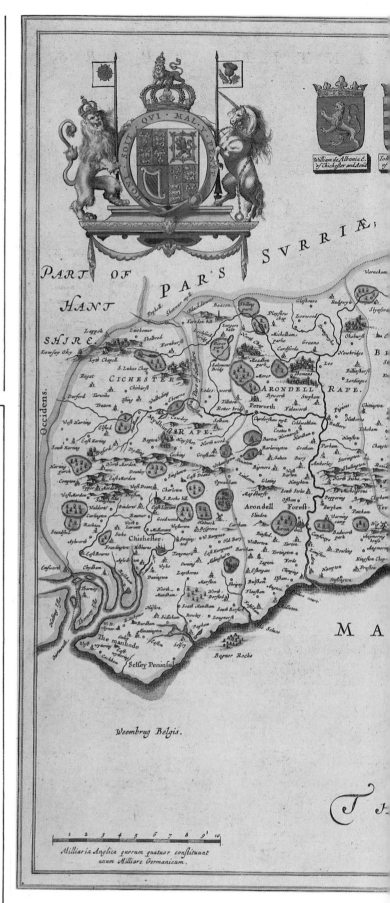

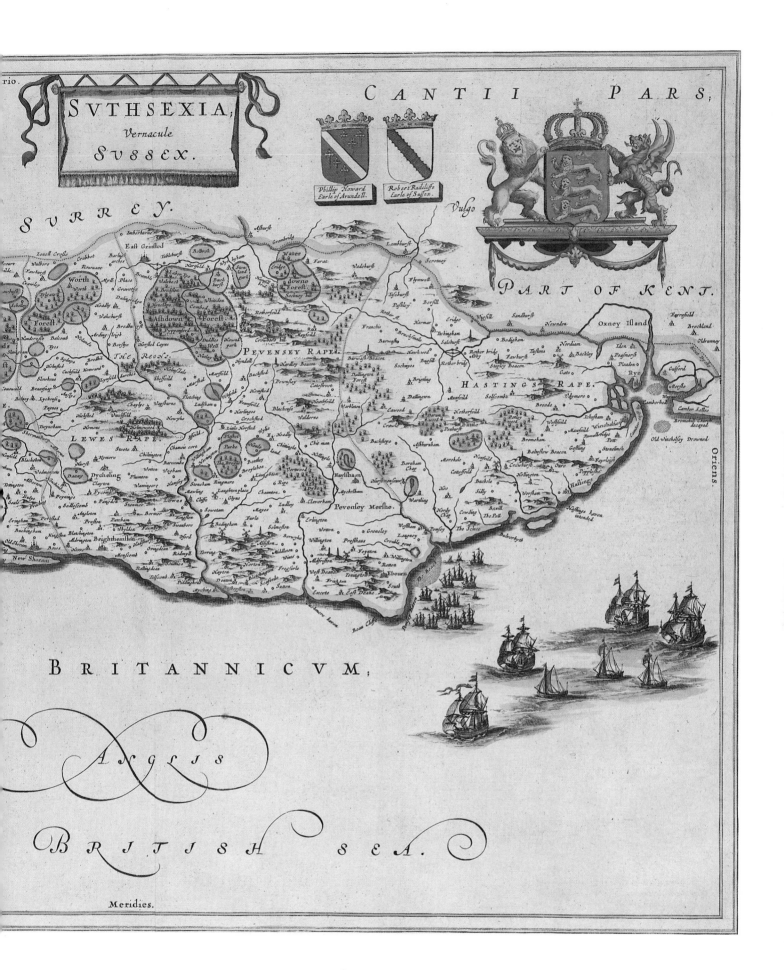

SVTHSEXIA,
Vernacule
SVSSEX.

Phillip Howard
Earle of Arundell.

Robert Radcliffe
Earle of Sussex.

CANTII   PARS,

Vulgo

PART OF KENT.

SVRREY.

Oriens.

BRITANNICVM,

ANGLIS

BRITISH   SEA.

Meridies.

Feuding and the Iron Industry

It was a triumph for the descendants of the Norman earls of the Rapes who lived in their big houses with French names like Hurstmonceux and Hurstpierpoint. They enjoyed a high standard of living, feasting and jousting, hunting, shooting and hawking. But the common people of Sussex, groaning under the feudal system, were still little more than serfs. When, in 1348, the plague hit Sussex (the 'Black Death') the suffering was considerable though not as great as in some counties. Villages were wiped off the county map leaving the parish church, round which they once nestled, in not so splendid isolation. Or the community moved to a more healthy site after the churchyard became choked with plague victims.

Better off than the toilers in the fields were the ironmasters and the men they employed on the furnaces they fired with the wood of the Sussex Weald and fed with the iron ore which lay so close beneath the surface in so many parts of the county. Ironworking in Sussex, particularly along the Forest Ridge in the eastern part of the county, began before the Roman Occupation and was developed throughout the second and third centuries. A Roman iron smelting furnace, a *ferraria* or bloomery, was found at Holbeamwood near Ticehurst in 1968. It was one of several in Sussex. Domesday Book however recorded only one ferraria for Wealden Iron – at East Grinstead. The main centres in Sussex came to be at Buxted, Burwash, Penhurst, Maresfield, Ashburnham, Hartfield and Etchingham, but the craft was not resurrected until the thirteenth century. In 1253 the Sheriff of Sussex was told to provide 30,000 horseshoes and 60,000 nails for the King's army. In 1300 the Guild of Ferrers of London complained that the iron rims which the smiths of the Weald were making for cartwheels were too short.

In the fourteenth century the demand was not so much for farm implements as weapons. In 1359 the French surprised Winchelsea, burnt most of it to the ground and ravaged the surrounding countryside. In 1377 they captured Rye, slaughtering (as Froissart recorded) 'without sparing man or woman.' When they attacked and destroyed Winchelsea again in 1380, England's rulers in London decided that England must be defended by the efforts of the whole country not just the Cinque Ports. To meet the threat implied by the assembly of a huge French army at Sluys poised for a full-scale invasion of England in 1385, a proclamation ordered everyone living within six miles of Rye to gather up their belongings and retire within the town walls.

The general feeling of discontent among the deprived rural community came to a head in the summer of 1381 when the peasants of southern England rose in revolt, not so much against the young king Richard II, as against his advisers, the lords spiritual and lay. Above all they objected to the Poll Tax levied on every head or 'poll' over the age of fifteen. The farmers and labourers of Sussex backed the demands of Wat Tyler of Dartford in neighbouring Kent, the leader of the Peasants Revolt, to be released from the state of slavery to which they had been reduced by the Norman conquerors and still had to suffer. They wanted to be able to pay their rent in money not work; to be free to buy and sell their produce where they wished.

The centre of the revolt in Sussex was at Arundel. The county's oppressed boors burnt the abbot's farm at Coombes and broke into the Earl of Arundel's castle at Lewes. Few of their demands were met, but after the rebellion in which Tyler was killed, relations between man and master were never quite the same. The unrest surfaced again some seventy years later in the even more serious uprising of the men of Kent and Sussex led by Jack Cade, a servant of Thomas Baron Dacre of Heathfield, a member of the Fiennes family who had come over with the Conqueror. Cade, who aimed at deposing the king and holding everything in common, marched on London with a contingent from Sussex which was joined by a posse from Kent. Yeoman John Cotyng was elected 'Captain' of Burwash (pronounced Burrish) and attempted to break up the abbot's fair. Cade was captured and executed, and those who followed him to the capital with such high hopes returned to the wheat fields of Brightling and Ringmer, Pulborough and Midhurst, with little chance of any

improvement in the nearly sub-human conditions which drove them to take up arms against their king.

Their suffering was aggravated by the continued need for stronger defence of the Sussex coast from the intensified attacks of the French, and the levying of a tax on all fish landed in order to pay for it. In 1448 the front line towns of Winchelsea and Rye were once more burnt to the ground by the French. The fact that their homes were in the county with the exposed flank which the French were apparently incapable of leaving in peace, seemed to condemn the farming and fishing communities of Sussex to perpetual poverty.

The Church

The lower ranks of the clergy were just as poor as the labourers, and still lived as a race apart. They rarely agreed with their superiors on points of doctrine, or with their parishioners, at a time when religion was an instrument of politics and public attendance at Christian worship a measure of loyalty to the Crown. The upper echelons of the priesthood in their turn held views often wildly out of step with those of *their* superiors. Heresy reached a high point in Sussex in 1457 with the publication of a book by the Bishop of Chichester which was immediately condemned by the head of the (Roman Catholic) Church in England as heretical and led to the author's humiliating recantation.

There was little reaction in Sussex to King Henry VIII's campaign against the monasteries which began with the Visitation to the county of Dr Richard Layton in 1535. Though when Bayham Abbey was suppressed in 1525, the local inhabitants had forcibly restored the canons for a period. The Vicar of Ticehurst, Thomas Cowley, continued to preach on miracles and images despite the king's injunction to change traditional attitudes and adjust their form of worship to suit his political ambition. On the other hand some Sussex priests indulged themselves by carrying out the royal commands with extreme zeal. In February 1536 the Rector of Graffham gave up making holy bread and holy water on Sundays and allowed his hair to grow to hide his tonsure. When in 1538 a decree came out condemning shrines and relics, the people of Sussex were as ardent as any others in throwing out altar stones with carved reredoses, defacing stained glass and making vestments into carpets.

With the accession of Catholic Queen Mary in 1553, of course, bewildered subjects were required to switch back to the Old Religion. In 1554 the Justices of Sussex received a letter from St James's Palace enjoining them to be more diligent in punishing 'evill ordered persones as used to raile upon the misteries of Christ's religion' – the brave people who could not in all conscience change back to the Roman rites 'at a stroke' with the same cynical facility as their neighbours, and were dubbed 'Protestants' to imply rebellion, disloyalty and all that was politically 'evil'. In June 1555 the new Authorities issued a writ for the burning of one Derrick Carver at Lewes, a Flemish brewer of Brighton, for 'heresy'. The following summer four were burned at Lewes for the same 'crime', and a month later another two. In June 1557 five men and five women were burnt to death in one fire at Lewes. One of them was Richard Woodham wealthy ironfounder of Warbleton.

Troubled Times

The products of the ironfounders were in great demand when England lost Calais to France in 1558, the year Queen Mary mercifully died, and the royal gun casting establishments were moved to Sussex. Measures had to be taken to prevent the ironworks and the cannons they produced from falling into the hands of the enemy. The primitive blooming process had given

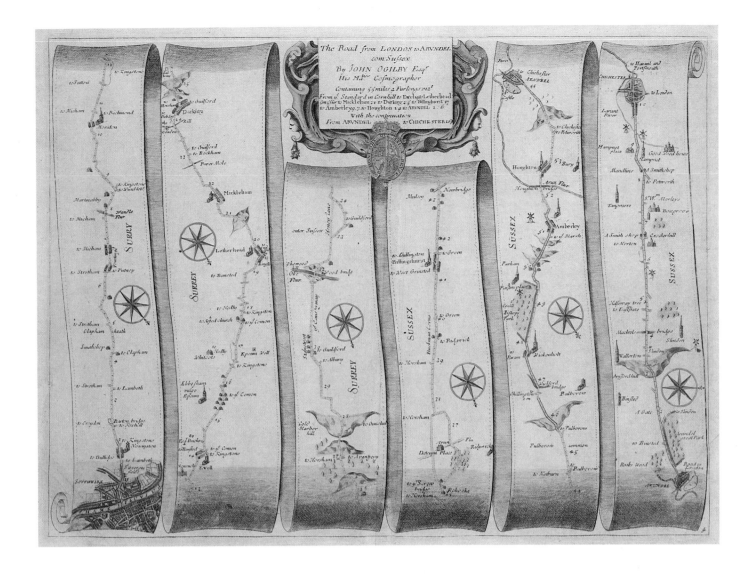

The Road from London to Arundel by John Ogilby c. 1675

'Rich is the soil and yeeldeth great plentie of all things necessarie, but very ill for travellers, especially in the Winter, the land lying low and the wayes very deep'. This is the description of Sussex by a seventeenth century mapmaker and surveyor. But despite his gloomy prediction there were travellers as this road map-one of the first ever published-illustrates. However, any kind of journey was still a hazard as the road surfaces were full of potholes and highwaymen were abroad.

This map of the road from London to Arundel and on to Chichester appeared in Ogilby's Britannia: Volume The First and is in a strip format still used occasionally today. He claimed to have measured all the roads of England and Wales with a waywiser and to have established the statute rule of 1,760 yards.

John Ogilby (1600–75) took up map publishing late in life after a variety of careers including dancing master and theatre owner. His first publishing business was destroyed in the Great Fire of London, 1666, but he built it up again and was appointed Royal Cosmographer. The first volume of Britannia contained 100 strip roads of journeys in England and Wales but the next projected two volumes never materialised as Ogilby died in 1675. Each of the strips contain a directional compass rose and distances are marked in miles and furlongs on a scale of one inch to the mile. Ogilby's work was extremely important and was used as a source of reference by later mapmakers who produced regional and county maps showing roads for the first time. (By courtesy of Baynton Williams, Old Maps, Prints and Books, Arundel, West Sussex)

way to blast furnaces early in the sixteenth century. Sir Henry Sidney had a furnace and forge near Robertsbridge Abbey in 1541, and two years later the first casting of an iron cannon took place at Buxted. However the first water hammer of the Weald had been set up in Newbridge as far back as 1492.

There had been rumours of a French landing in Sussex in 1586, but the enemy who were now expected to make the most determined attack were the Spanish. When their preparations for an Armada were seen to be in earnest, Queen Elizabeth raised a Sussex force to defend the coast—4,000 foot soldiers and 260 horses. Batteries were set up and troops lined along the shore. Block houses were built at Brighton to prevent a repeat of the conflagration started by the French in 1545. But when, on 28 July 1588 the Spanish Armada passed the Sussex coast without so much as firing a token broadside, the county force was disbanded. With the defeat of Spain the casting of iron guns in Sussex temporarily ceased. Sussex rustics were not cut out for the military life and welcomed the stand down as the end of soldiering for the time being. But they reckoned without the anti-Catholic fervour of Good Queen Bess who felt it incumbent on her to send a force to aid the Protestant King Henry IV of France. In 1589 a thousand men of Sussex found themselves embarking at Rye Harbour for the coast of France. They arrived so badly equipped that Lord Buckhurst had to rearm them from his own armoury, and wrote to the Sussex justices asking them to explain how they came to send so ill-armed a selection of loose and ragged fellows.

Herbrand de Saqueville came to England in William's army of conquest and was holding land in England in 1094. Before acquiring Knole, their huge house in Kent in 1603, the Sackville family lived at Buckhurst near Rotherfield in Sussex in a mansion which came into their hands in the reign of Henry II. It was Queen Elizabeth who created Thomas Sackville Baron Buckhurst.

Disloyalty and loyalty were now measured in terms of dissent from and conforming with the prevailing, or 'orthodox', version of Christian worship which was anti-Papist, anti-Priest. Protestantism was no longer a dirty word, but Queen Elizabeth was anxious to keep a balance and not encourage extremists of either persuasion. Non-conformity with the tenets of the new Church *of* England (no longer *in* England) appeared in Sussex in 1576 when one Dick Thickpenny, a Brighton curate, was suspended by his bishop on suspicion of being a member of a sect called The Family of Love, for having ministered without wearing a surplice and having contempt for the Church of England's Authority. In 1583 six Sussex clergy refused to sign the thirty-nine articles of Religion agreed at the Convocation of 1562 'for avoiding the Diversities of opinions and for the establishing of consent touching true religion.'

In 1591 the Mayor of Rye remonstrated that 'now of late a small secte of puritanes more holy in shewe than in dede is sprung up amongst us' and proscribed 'certain mutynous fellowes of this towne who professe to be more pure than others.' The acts of those who sought to restore the version which had prevailed before Henry VIII had broken with the Pope, were regarded as 'treason' and punishable by death. There was a desperate hunt in the Sussex sea towns at the time of the Armada to flush out priests who were suspected of welcoming the Spanish and giving them horses if they landed, and in August 1588 Edward Shelley of the distinguished Sussex family was hanged at Tyburn. John Oven was arrested at Battle at about the same time, with three others, accused of being a seminary priest and of treason. He pleaded guilty to the former but not the latter. He was however convicted of both, and on hearing the sentence his courage failed him and he agreed to take the Oath of Supremacy and to renounce the Pope and his doctrines; but the others were duly hanged. Scotney Castle near Lamberhurst, the seat of the Darell family, was twice searched by priest hunters. Though now in Kent, in the sixteenth century it was in Sussex; until changed in 1897, the county boundary followed the original course of the River Bewl. For seven years from 1591 to 1598 the castle was the secret centre for the missionary activities of Father Richard Blount, and it was this determined Jesuit for whom they hunted. Thomas Darell II and his servants were removed to Newgate gaol while the search was on, and his wife and children confined to one room. But they failed to discover the hole near the staircase in which the priest and his companion were hiding. Blount escaped during a planned diversion on their second visit in 1598.

In the troubled times of the Great Rebellion the men of East Sussex sided for the most part with the Parliamentarians who held all the Cinque Ports and Lewes. In the western part of the county, however, the royalist gentry were very strong and kept Arundel Castle for King Charles. In 1648 the knights, gentry and clergy of Sussex—in particular the Cavaliers of Horsham—petitioned Parliament that the captured king should be treated with the respect due to his rank. When the King's son, Charles Edward Prince of Wales, survived the defeat of the royalist army at Worcester in 1651, his difficulty in finding a way to escape to the continent was solved, after wanderings in a variety of disguises, by a Brighton skipper Captain Tettersell. Colonel Gounter got him to take the Prince on board his sailing boat at Shoreham with the cover story of a man evading the law after having fought a duel. From this small Sussex harbour the Prince sailed in safety to Fécamp. With his return to England as King Charles II nine years later, it was for the Sussex supporters of the Usurper Cromwell to make the voyage to France—and America.

But they were in a minority. Most stayed, and those in the 'perverse' towns of Chichester and Lewes continued to demonstrate their Puritanism without however entering whole-heartedly into the scheming of the likes of Titus Oates, the fanatical Protestant priest who pretended he had unearthed a Jesuit plot to kill Charles II which, until it was revealed as an invention, resulted in the execution of thirty-five innocent citizens. Oates was a Sussex man, the son of the rector of All Saints Church, Hastings.

Many were unable to condone the popular delusion that demented old women were in league with evil spirits if not Old Nick himself, and though unable to save Ann Taylor of Rye from being condemned to death for witchcraft, managed to secure her reprieve on account of her pregnancy. They found it difficult to tolerate the followers of George Fox, the mockingly called Quakers, who got a grip on a certain section of the Sussex community. With his companion Alexander Parker, Fox made a short tour of Sussex and held meetings in Steyning, Lewes and Warbleton. Many other itinerant Quaker preachers came to Sussex such as Thomas Robinson who, at a meeting in Southover in 1655 is said to have made many converts. But they upset many others by rudely disrupting other people's meetings, entering non-dissenting churches in the middle of their services and starting to argue with the preacher. One of them marched into Burwash church and challenged the vicar Thomas Goldham in his own pulpit. They courted unpopularity among the roughneck farming community by refusing to swear or to pay their tithes. Other extremists like Walter Postlethwait of St Michael's, Lewes 'in the Fifth Monarchy notion,' in 1658 tried to persuade his friends to join him in signing a Confession of Faith in London, far removed from the Thirty Nine Articles. On the restoration of the King, however, he agreed to conform. A hundred years later John Wesley had little influence in Sussex, making only short visits to Rye and Winchelsea in 1773 and 1790.

More disruptive to Sussex life than the inconsequential debates on the merits of the various forms of Christian worship and belief were the raids made on the Sussex coast by French privateers, mostly from Dunkirk. They had increased during the Civil War since all naval protection was withdrawn. In 1652 things got so bad that the fisherman of Brighton petitioned Parliament. In times of peace, they said, they were wont to have and employ at sea sixty fishing barks which earned them £8,000 a year.

> But now, within these last three years or four years, by the force and rage of their enemies, the Dunkerks and French men of war, they have been debarred of their former fishing voyages, and the sea hath been shut up from them, so that they could not go about their former affairs and have been hindered to the value of £30,000; fourteen of the best barkes of their town have been taken and carried away by the enemy, most of them laden with merchandise, and many of their poore neighbours have been chased ashore and pillaged by them who have stript and taken from them that little parcel which they had.

Chart of the Approach to Rye by Captain Greenvile Collins, 1693

This lovely chart of the approach to Rye appeared in Great Britain's Coasting Pilot, *the first marine atlas of British waters engraved and printed in London from original surveys. Until the publication of this atlas British sailors had been relying mainly on Dutch charts of the home coastline. The Dutch wars accentuated the need for British charts and in 1681, Charles II announced that he had appointed 'Captain Collins Commander of the Merlin Yacht to make a survey of the seacoasts of the Kingdom by measuring all the Sea coasts with a chain and taking all the bearings of the headlands . . .' This formidable task was completed in eight years from 1681 to 88 and the* Coasting Pilot *was the result.*

Captain Collins was an officer in the Royal Navy and was master of the frigate Charles from 1676 to 1679. He surveyed the English coast in two different ships—the Merlin *and the* Monmouth—*and the whole exercise took about seven years. (By courtesy of Cartographia, Southampton Street, London)*

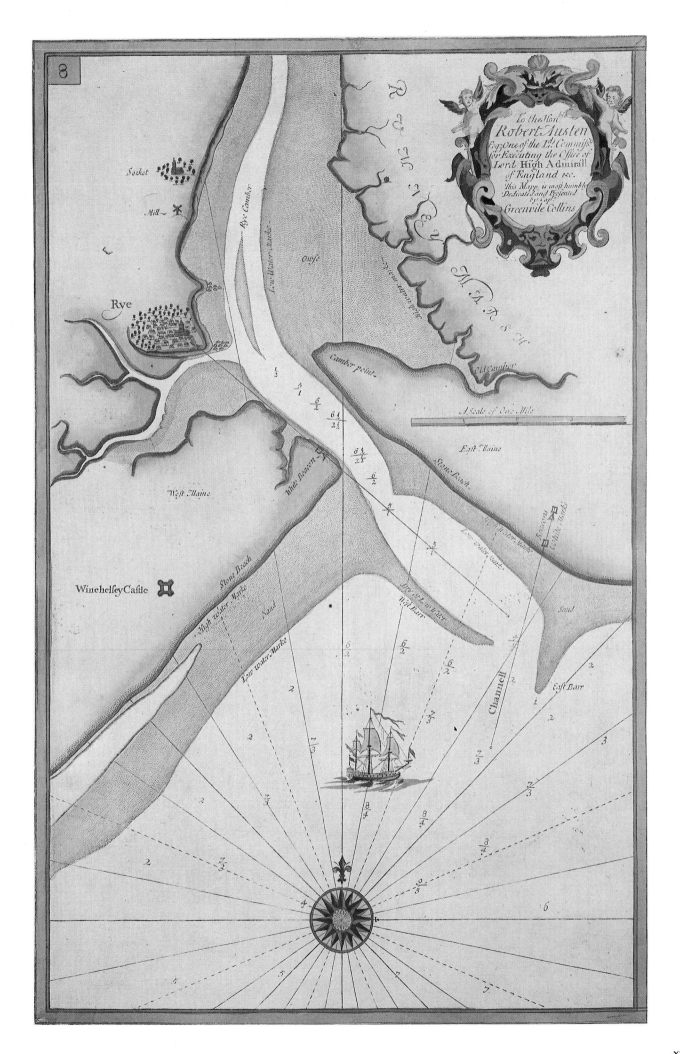

Smugglers Abound

It was in this year of 1652 that the author of the only classic literary work of enduring fame produced in the county, Thomas Otway, was born at Trotton in Sussex. His blank verse tragedy *Venice Preserved* written in 1682, was described by Emile Legouis in his *History of English Literature* as 'a unique achievement . . . a solitary work unequalled in the half century which preceded it or the century which came after.' Otway's father was Rector of Woolbeding.

For the peaceful citizens of Sussex the fights between smugglers and the excise men, and among rival gangs, was as much a curse as piracy—to say nothing of the activities of horse stealers, cattle thieves and highwaymen. When Horace Walpole stayed at a hotel in Robertsbridge in 1749 he found it full of smugglers. Export smugglers were known as 'free traders'. Illicitly exporting wool from Sussex had begun in the middle of the thirteenth century. From 1341 Winchelsea and Rye were named as the two ports from which wool could be exported legally on payment of a duty of 50s a sack, and licences were given to those who were prepared to act within the law in this way. Weaving wool took place in Sussex in the mid-sixteenth century, and to improve their cloth making techniques Queen Elizabeth encouraged the immigration of better trained foreign weavers. The restored King Charles II prohibited the export of wool altogether, and in 1662 it was made a felony. So the illicit shipping of wool out of Sussex by Englishmen who loaded bags of it on to waiting French ships began in earnest. Known as 'owling', it continued into the first quarter of the nineteenth century.

Smuggling *into* Sussex started at the beginning of the seventeenth century with Lyons silk and Valenciennes lace being landed at Seaford, Newhaven and Shoreham. It reached a peak in the eighteenth century, not only in 'fine goods' but tobacco, tea and spirits. According to a report of 1703 the fifty 'ryding-officers', appointed by the Government to guard the coasts of Kent and Sussex from the Isle of Sheppy of Ensworth, made little

impact on the owlers—by now the word was being applied to all nocturnal smugglers. As William Cooper related in 1858,

> The new force was utterly inadequate to the suppression of the trade. In the next forty-five years the daring of the smugglers grew with the impunity with which they were enabled to act. Large gangs of twenty, forty, fifty and even one hundred rode, armed with guns, bludgeons and clubs, throughout the country, setting every one at defiance and awing all the quiet inhabitants. They established ware-houses and vaults in many districts for the reception of their goods, and built large houses at Seacock's Heath, in Etchingham (built by the well-known smuggler Arthur Gray and called 'Gray's Folly'), at Pix Hall and the Four Throws, Hawkhurst, at Goudhurst and elsewhere, with the profits of their trade.

Tea was a much prized commodity. In June 1733 officers of the customs at Newhaven tried to seize ten horses laden with tea at Cuckmere, but they were confronted by some thirty owlers armed with pistols and blunderbusses who fired on the officers and held them prisoner while they escaped with the tea. A similar incident happened that August at Greenhay. The customs officers were often assisted by dragoons but as occurred one December night in 1735 they were unable to prevent a large gang of smugglers surrounding the representatives of law and order and confining them for an hour and a half while they made off.

They were a ruthless and bloodthirsty lot and gave no quarter.

On 13 June 1744 customs officers from Eastbourne went with five mounted dragoons to Pevensey where they had been told a gang of smugglers were off loading spirits. They were soon surrounded by a hundred owlers who quickly disarmed them and then fired forty shots at them point blank. They ended, as William Cooper tells, by 'cutting them with swords in a dangerous manner, loading the goods on above one hundred horses and making towards London.'

For smugglers who were caught, tried, and found guilty the sentence was death. One William Pring was convicted at East Grinstead assizes,

> and there hung on 12 August, 1749, being conducted to the place of execution by a guard of soldiers, as a rescue was feared from the smugglers; and after execution he was hung in chains on Slindon Common. Others of the gang were tried at the same assizes as highwaymen and executed.

Hanging the bodies in chains in prominent places was meant as a deterrent, but the highwaymen, smugglers and horse stealers continued to go about their business with little regard for the peace and safety of their fellow citizens. So law-abiding farmers and landowners formed themselves into Proscecution Societies such as the one whose printed notice dated 1783 still hangs in the saloon bar of The Bell Hotel, Ticehurst. Its purpose was to raise a fund 'for prosecuting Persons who shall be found guilty of robbing or defrauding any Member of their property and that such offenders may be discovered and brought to justice.' There were thirty-five members, including two women, who each paid two shillings every six months until the stock was £50. Every member who had been robbed or defrauded (except in gaming) was obliged to give notice to the Society's clerk, and the committee would then decide if the offender would be prosecuted. The funds were spent on the cost of prosecution but also on rewards for those who laid information.

A Reward of Ten Pounds on the Conviction of any Person wilfully murdering any member of this society or stealing a horse or horses belonging to a member of this society.

Another reward given to apprehenders of horse stealers and other criminals in Sussex (and elsewhere) who were not members of a prosecuting Society was a Tyburn Ticket, a certificate given under the hand of an assize judge granting exemption for offices in the parish where the crime was committed.

Industry and Agriculture

Though the last smuggler was shot and killed near Rye in 1831, the running of contraband remained a sport along the Sussex coast for some time afterwards, and coastguard patrols continued to pace the cliffs from an hour before sunset to an hour after sunrise armed with pistols cutlass and portfire, and guided by the white chalk heaps which marked the cliff paths. Tom Paine, the author of *The Rights of Man,* was an Excise Man at Lewes.

For each side aggressive ironmongery was easy to come by, since in the eighteenth century Sussex once again became a centre of gun-founding. In 1607 there had still been 140 hammers and furnaces in the county, but between the reign of Queen Elizabeth 1 and the Civil War there was little demand for guns. In any case, most of the trees in the Weald had been cut down for fuel and there was not all that amount of water to work the hammers which beat the ingots into shape. The problem of substituting sea coal or pit coal for the more costly charcoal was solved and, as a result, Budgen's Sussex map of 1724 showed only fifteen furnaces and ten forges. Abraham Darby's success with coal-fired furnaces at Coalbrook in Shropshire finally put paid to the charcoal-fired Sussex iron industry, though there was still a furnace working at Ashburnham as late as 1825. For the first half of the eighteenth century, however, the Fullers of Brightling Park near Heathfield conducted iron-smelting and gun-making on a big scale. They not only made guns for the Ordnance but also for private and foreign customers such as the King of Sardinia. The finished guns were taken to Brandbridges on the Medway in a cart drawn by oxen, and from there conveyed to their customers by sea. These Sussex blast furnaces were fired by coal acquired outside the county, of course, but the locally dug iron ore was often burnt with charcoal before being introduced to the furnace to break it down into smaller pieces.

The Fullers (family motto 'Carbone et Forcibus'—by Charcoal and Tongs) date back as a Sussex family to 1575, and as early as 1650 one of them acquired the lease of Cheddingly stream furnace. In 1693 John Fuller acquired the Brightling site for the iron-making business on which the family fortunes were founded. His son married the daughter of a wealthy English planter in the West Indies and managed the business till his death in 1745. The third generation in the guise of Rose Fuller, the *son* of John Fuller II in spite of his Christian name, carried on until his death in 1777. The business was then run by his nephew 'Mad John Fuller' MP who was expelled from the House of Commons for being drunk, restored Bodiam Castle and built himself a pyramid tomb in the graveyard of Brightling Church. But by then the Fuller gun-founding business was a dying activity. The guns on Nelson's ships were 'carronades' made by The Carron Company in Falkirk, Scotland, which had opened in 1760, and so were the guns which defended the forts on the West Indian islands and pointed across the English Channel from the Martello Towers built to protect the Sussex coast from invasion by the troop-laden barges which Napoleon had assembled at Boulogne. But maybe some of Fuller's armoury was deployed behind the 20-yard-wide and 23-mile-long Military Canal running from Cliffe End near Rye to Shorne Cliffe in adjoining Kent, dug to stop the French getting a foothold and advancing into the interior. At a meeting in the White Hart in Lewes in 1779 plans were laid to raise twenty-four companies of a Sussex Militia composed entirely of men of the county—with the gentry as officers and farmers as sergeants— and they drew up a programme of military training and shooting practice, with prizes for the best performers. Each village held a ballot to decide which of their menfolk aged between 18 and 45 would constitute the parish's quota for five year's service in the Militia.

Sussex by Schenck and Valk c. 1695

The end of the seventeenth century saw a lull in the development of British mapmaking apart from the publication of John Ogilby's road atlas and the sea atlas of Captain Greenvile Collins. The large Dutch publishing companies of Willem Blaeu and his great rival, Jan Jansson, were also in decline but Janson's engraved plates were bought in auction by Pieter Schenk and Gerald Valk, also Dutch publishers, who reissued the maps with some alterations. Sussex is one of these and Janson's inprint can still be seen at the bottom of the map.

The rural industries of the county are represented on the cartouche in the form of a cow and a sheep and its maritime nature by Neptune and his companions who seem to be enjoying quite a party with some amazing sea monsters! (By courtesy of Ivan Deverall, Maps and Prints, Cambridge Way, Uckfield, Sussex)

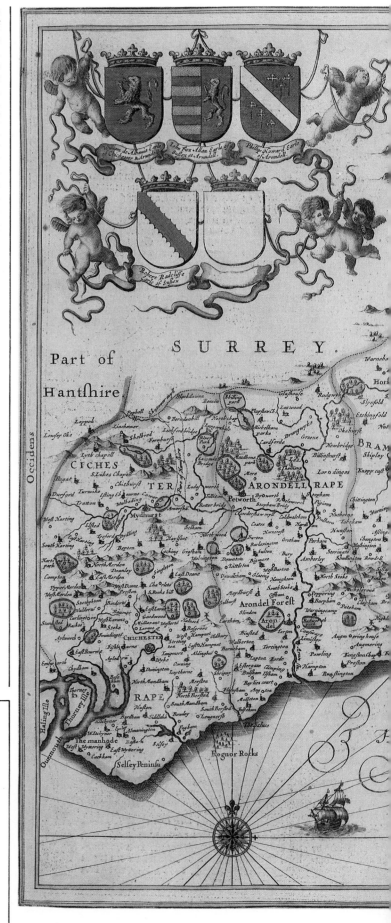

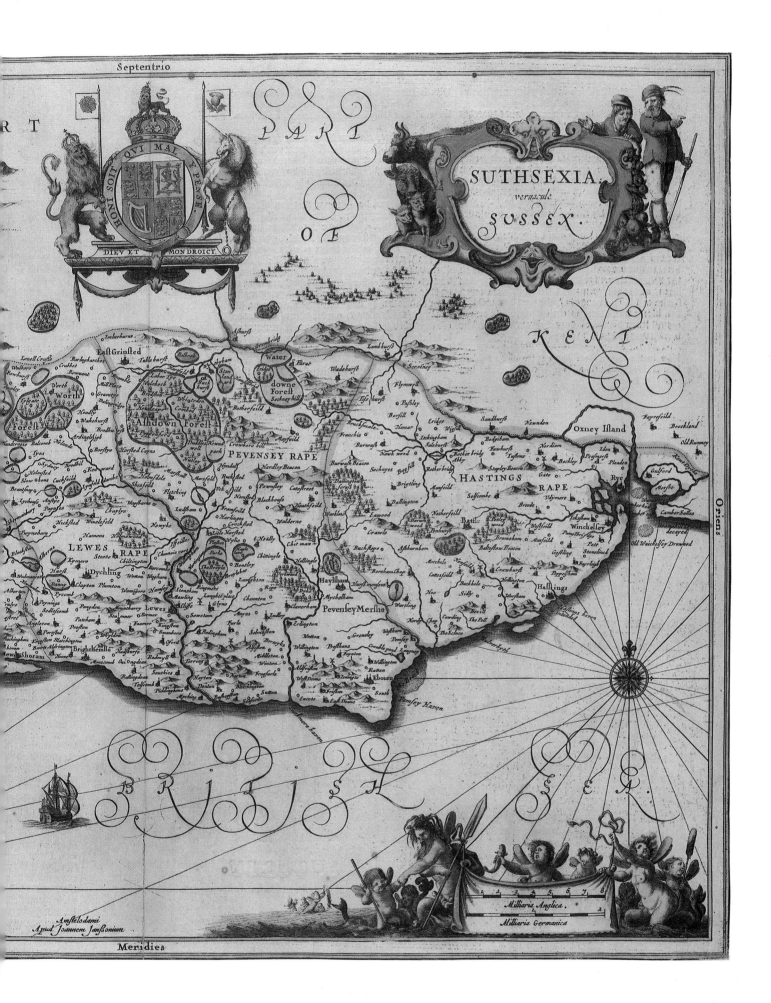

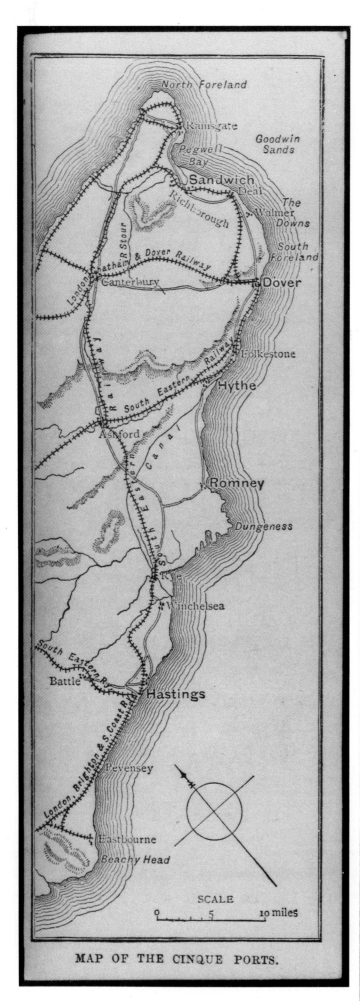

MAP OF THE CINQUE PORTS.

Many French families who fled the terror of the French Revolution came to live in Sussex—some 1,100 refuges arrived in 1792 alone—but when George III declared war against the armies formed to spread the revolution to countries outside France, these potential enemies of the King were made to leave the coast and were settled further inland at Lindfield and Cuckfield. A British camp was put down at Brighton in 1793 which, within a year, was accommodating 15,000 troops; various army units were stationed in other Sussex towns. In 1795 volunteers were asked for the Midhurst, Lewes and Western Coast Yeomanry Cavalry, the Goodwood Volunteer Horse Artillery, the Arundel and Bramber Yeomanry Cavalry and similar amateur units. The danger of invasion by the French was greatest between 1803 and 1804. A landing was expected at the place which the Normans had chosen 800 years before, Pevensey Bay, where sluices were arranged for flooding. Another army camp was formed at Eastbourne. Some ninety-four 24-pound guns were lined up between Seaford and the Kent border.

This considerable defence force was stood down in 1805 when it seemed that a landing was unlikely. As a result, the demand for the warlike products of the gun-founders of Brightling, and the gun-powder makers of Battle, fell away. The more peaceful crafts of glass making, bell founding, paper and rope making continued to flourish in a small way, but the main role of Sussex was to provide food for the ever growing city of London.

Up to the middle of the eighteenth century wool had been the chief source of profit to English farmers. A sheep's fleece was golden, its carcase of little value. In the selection of rams and ewes for breeding the choice had been determined by consideration of their coats, but now mutton was to be more greatly prized than the fineness of wool. The man who developed the transition was the Leicestershire farmer Robert Bakewell who 'provided meat for the million and by so doing contributed as much to the wealth of the country as Arkwright or Watt.' He bred sheep which weighed most in the best joints and quickly repaid the cost of the food they consumed—'small in size and great in value.' For a time Bakewell's New Leicesters swept all competitors before them, but his example was quickly followed by other breeders. As one historian has put it,

> As the New Leicesters had been improved till they held the rich plains against all comers, so the Southdowns for the hills and the Cheviots for the mountains were improved by breeders who followed the example of Bakewell. As the pioneer of stock-breeding the Leicestershire farmer may be considered in a sense the creator of the Southdown of Ellman of Glynde.

The Southdown breed of sheep was certainly as famous as the Leicestershire sheep, and by now emulated them for the excellence of their mutton. In his 1839 Sussex Directory, Pigot boasted, 'Southdowns have deservedly become the favourite breed all over the island.'

Thomas Ellman lived in a house near Glynde Place, but his son moved to Firle and his grandson lived in the Manor, Southover, outside Lewes. Both Glynde and Southover were within riding distance of Brighton where the court often met during the Regency. The regent's brother used to ride over to see the Ellmans at Glynde once a week to get away from the tedium of the court—HRH Prince Augustus Frederick, sixth son of George III, born 1773, who was created Duke of Sussex in 1801.

But it was the fertile soil of Sussex, not its pasturage, from which the growing population of London—the Great Wen as William Cobbett called it—derived so much sustenance. Coming to Singleton on the turnpike road between Midhurst and Chichester on one of his Rural Rides in 1822, Cobbett wrote that

> The lane goes along through some of the finest farms in the world. It is impossible for corn land and for agriculture to be finer than these.

Up to 1760 England produced enough corn to feed the whole population and have some left over to sell abroad. In 1700 the population of England and Wales had been around five and a half million, but by 1800 it was more than nine million. The Great Wen had become proportionately greater as the villages became

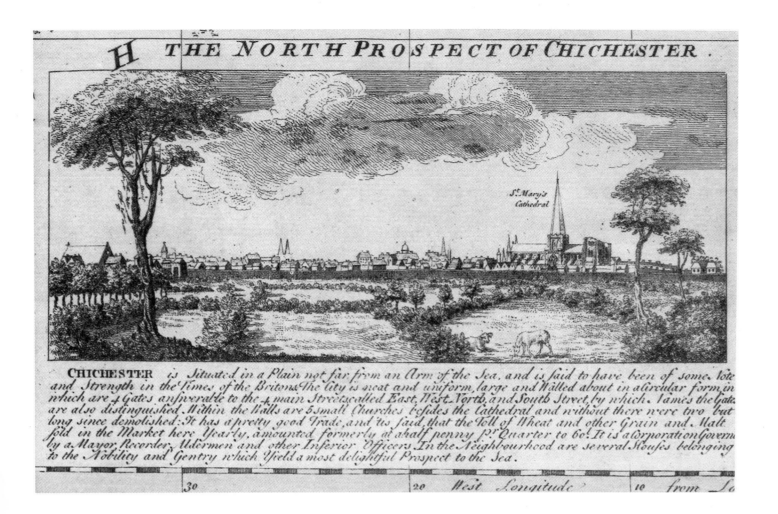

THE NORTH PROSPECT OF CHICHESTER.

St. Mary's Cathedral

CHICHESTER *is Situated in a Plain not far from an Arm of the Sea, and is said to have been of some Note and Strength in the Times of the Britons. The City is neat and uniform, large and Walled about in a circular form, in which are 4 Gates answerable to the 4 main Streets called East, West, North, and South Street, by which. James the Gate. are also distinguished. Within the Walls are 5 small Churches besides the Cathedral and without there were two but long since demolished. It has a pretty good Trade, and 'tis said, that the Toll of Wheat and other Grain and Malt sold in the Market here Yearly, amounted formerly at a half penny P.* Quarter to 60£. It is a Corporation Governed by a Mayor, Recorder, Aldermen and other Inferior Officers. In the Neighbourhood are several Houses belonging to the Nobility and Gentry which Yield a most delightful Prospect to the Sea.*

30   20   *West Longitude*   10   *from L*

A view of the walled city of Chichester taken from Emanuel Bowen's map of Sussex published in The Large English Atlas, 1749–60. (By courtesy of Ivan Deverall, Maps and Prints, Cambridge Way, Uckfield, Sussex)

deserted. And so the corn fields of Sussex, Kent and Essex and the other Home Counties could no longer produce the grain for loaves to feed the people of London and themselves. The shortage brought high prices for producers and the war with France cut the country off from European supplies. The freehold yeomen, tenant farmers and receivers of tithe and rent in Sussex prospered but the poor, whose survival depended on getting their daily bread suffered terribly—they just could not afford the inflated price. Wheat rose from 43 shillings a quarter in 1792 to 126 in 1812. When the price fell after Waterloo many farmers found themselves unable to maintain their high standard of living and could not pay their rent. But Parliament was on *their* side, not the consumers. The Corn Law which the legislators passed in 1815 was blatantly aimed at restoring agricultural prosperity at the expense of the consumer. The people of the towns for whom the high price of bread had to continue made no bones of their resentment of the wealth and luxury of the Landed Gentry. But seven years after the peace and the passing of the Corn Law, Willian Cobbett considered the lot of the Sussex labourer a happy one when compared with that of the factory worker in the north.

There is *no misery* to be seen here [Petworth]. I have seen no wretchedness in Sussex; nothing to be at all compared to that which I have seen in other parts; and as to these villages in the South Downs they are beautiful to behold (*Rural Rides*, 1822)

Every inch of the land which he rode through that Saturday morning of 2 August 1822, noted William Cobbett, belonged either to the Duke of Richmond (of Goodwood) or to Lord Egremont (of Petworth)—and no harm in that if those who tilled the land had fair play, which Cobbett considered they had. But within a few years the Mobbing Winter of 1830 was upon them with violent protest against widespread Agricultural Distress.

When the euphoria over the defeat of Emperor of the French had died, the long awaited peace brought nothing but misery. Winning the war brought creeping economic depression which came to a head between 1830 and 1835. Members of Parliament in far away London learnt of the extent of the distress when their Commission of Enquiry reported that 'thousands of persons are living on twopence halfpenny a day.' There had been a series of bad harvests, and manual labour was being replaced by steam driven machinery. The men and women of Sussex, whose hands were no longer needed to gather in the harvest, were sent into the fields to pick stones. The anger and hatred against the Sheens was vented in an orgy of smashing, rioting and burning by organised mobs whose ringleaders terrorised Sussex prowling the villages for recruits. Many who thought they were safely hidden from the mobbers were forced to join them against their will. Jack Robinson, a hoop shaver of Itchingfield, feared he would lose his old soldier's pension if he went with them and climbed into the roof of his workshop on their approach. He only came out when they started chopping his shed down. When Abraham Weller of Warnham refused to join them, they tore his clothes, seized a horse and cart and chained him to it dragging him at the cart's tail till he shouted he was willing to do as they asked. The rick fires they started at Redhill, Eastbourne, Battle and Horsham could be seen for miles around, and left no one in doubt that they would stop at nothing to draw attention to their despair.

Many Labourers' Unions—legal since 1825—were formed in Sussex. The Horsham branch of the National Political Union had 700 members. They were inducted at a mock ceremonial swearing-in, presided over by a Chief Officer wearing a white surplice with a belt and sword, designed to frighten feeble-minded ploughmen into committing every kind of crime for fear of the consequences of disobedience. One-time smugglers knew the way of getting people to work together in gangs, and gave the lead to the unemployed farm workers of the kind that had combined at Shipley, the most notorious Union of them all.

Out of sympathy with their unhappy lot, many Sussex juries at Quarter Sessions found rioters not guilty when the evidence quite obviously pointed the other way. Numbers of middle class residents and tradesmen of Horsham found the extreme actions of the distressed workers justified by the extreme nature of the provocation, and refused to be sworn in as special constables. To counter this apathy, if not collusion, of the amateur law enforcers who were themselves part of the community over whom they had to pass judgement, East Sussex was one of the first counties to adopt paid constables when the County Police Act of 1839 recommended the formation of a new professional Police Force.

The situation became more tense towards the end of the 1830s as more and more joined the movement to force the repeal of the Corn Law of 1815 which prohibited the import of foreign corn and was responsible for keeping bread at a price only the well-to-do could afford. Leading the defenders of the status quo was the aristocratic Duke of Richmond, the Farmers' Friend, and President of the Society for the Protection of Agriculture who spoke at meetings all over Sussex. But he was no match for his opponent Richard Cobden, another man of Sussex born at Heyshott in 1804 and a pupil at Midhurst Grammar School. In 1838, following two bad harvests Cobden formed the Anti-Corn Law League, a pressure group which gained the support of the entire new middle class. When he died in 1865 he was buried at Lavington, happy in the knowledge that Free Trade was a reality and the exhortation contained in his broadsheet ballads had been heeded.

> The haughty possess the land,
>   And wield oppression's rod,
> In spite of that divine command
>   Found in the word of God;
> The Corn Laws petrify their hearts
>   And make the nation groan,
> For when the people cry for bread
>   They only get a stone.
>
> Then open every British port
>   And let the poor be fed,
> No longer see your children starve
>   And die through want of bread.

Many felt there was more to be repealed than the Corn Law—which did not happen until 1846. Political reform as well as economic change was sought by those for whom the great Reform Act of 1832 did not go far enough.

For centuries Sussex had returned twenty-eight members to the House of Commons, but the famous 1832 measure disenfranchised five of its constituencies, Bramber, East Grinstead, Seaford, Steyning and Winchelsea the rotten borough where Henry Brougham had been the member. So then the county's representation at Westminster for its 272,300 population, 297 parishes and twenty market towns was down to eighteen. The Reform Act gave it two county members for each of its two divisions, east and west, and two each for Chichester, Hastings, Brighton, New Shoreham and Lewes. Voters at Rye, Arundel, Horsham and Midhurst returned one each. In spite of the changes politics was still the occupation of the haughty. The members for West Sussex were Lord George Lennox and the Earl of Surrey; the single member for Arundel Lord Fitzalan, grandson of the Duke of Norfolk; one of the two Chichester MPs was Lord Arthur Lennox and one of the members for East Sussex was Hon Compton Cavendish. Brighton became a borough in 1832 and one of its members was Sir Adolphus Dalyrymple. From their point of vantage in the House of Lords the county's great landowners, the Duke of Richmond, the Duke of Norfolk,

the Earl of Egremont, Lord Ashburnham and the Earl of Chichester saw there was no decline in the respect paid to property.

Shoreham had been represented in Parliament for 540 years—Inigo Jones the architect had been its MP from 1620 to 1621—and did not lose its seat until 1885 when, under the Redistribution of Seats Act, it was merged with Lewes. At the 1826 election three candidates fought for the two 'rotten' constituencies of the Rape of Bramber and the Borough of Shoreham, and between them they spent £6,000. Because its electors were so scattered, Shoreham was exempted from the provision of the 1832 Reform Act which made it unlawful for any money to be disbursed for conveying voters to the poll.

Those who wanted universal suffrage, annual parliaments and a secret ballot listed their proposals in the Charter which gave them their name and held gatherings all over England. Chartism, promoted by manual workers, did not find general favour in Sussex. When in September 1839 the retiring mayor of Chichester, Mr Irving, let the town hall for a Chartist meeting he was soundly reproved. He defended his action by saying that if being a Chartist meant the endeavour to remove abuses and corruptions in the Church and State he was willing to be so considered.

The Coming of the Railway

The landscape too was being subjected to upheaval—and in a way changed social attitudes and habits as much as any law. In 1815 an Act of Parliament had been obtained to cut a Portsmouth–Arundel Canal which went from the river Arun below Arundel to the estuary of the river Lavant (Chichester Harbour) through the channels which separated Thorney and Hayling Island to the east of Portsea Island and on to Portsmouth. In 1825 a Baybridge Canal Company had been formed to make a cut from Binesbridge to Baybridge. But two years before that the engineers Sir John Rennie and Robert Stephenson proposed linking London, Shoreham, Rochester and Portsmouth, with a branch to Brighton, by the revolutionary means of transport which had recently been tested in the north, an iron railway on which would run a steam locomotive drawing a train of carriages for passengers. It was the first of many schemes which they proposed in the south, including The Grand Southern Railway (known as 'Stephenson's Railway') which they surveyed from London through Dorking, Horsham and Shoreham to Brighton. A large building known as The Pioneer was built opposite Tan Yard footpath in Horsham as a prospective railway hotel, later known as Sussex House. But the plan fell through for both these since the prices asked for the land were higher than those for the Three Bridges scheme finally adopted. In 1837 the Surrey, Sussex, Hants, Wilts and Somerset Railway Company changed its name to the London and Brighton Railway Company, and work began in July 1838 on the section of the line between Brighton and Shoreham. It was ready for the first train to pass over on 11 May, 1840. It puffed out of Brighton station to music from a Lancers Band. The journey took 11½ minutes and people waved and cheered as it clattered past them. A regular service began at eight o'clock the next morning, and the main portion was being built through the Downs during 1839 and 1840. When it was completed it replaced Brighton's only means of communication with the metropolis which had been the horse and coach.

In 1839 twenty-three coaches left Brighton every day for London, but by 1841, when the complete railway was opened, there were only four. Four years later there was only one, the Victoria. Railway passengers came down from London in two hours at a cost of six shillings instead of five hours on the outside of a coach costing them 13 shillings. The new, fast, cheap service brought a new type of visitor, from a rougher section of the community, and in a few years had changed the character of Brighton completely.

Published by W. Grant News Agent 5. Castle Square.

View of the Railway Terminus Brighton

The Fashionable Resort

Royal patronage of Brighton began in 1782 when the Duke of Cumberland, the youngest and worst behaved of George III's brothers, acquired a small house in the town for himself and his consort the beautiful Mrs Horton. Ever since Dr Russell had moved there in 1750, Brighton had gathered a reputation as a fashionable sea-side resort for London Society, at which ladies and gentlemen could spend a summer holiday as a change from inland spas such as Tunbridge Wells or Bath. In 1761 someone described it as 'one of the principal resorts of the idle and dissipated.' Dr Samuel Johnson paid the place a brief visit in 1782 accompanied by Madame d'Arblay (Fanny Burney), Mrs Thrale and the three Miss Thrales, and insisted on finding out for himself why anyone should ever want to bathe in the sea.

The Duke of Cumberland was not on speaking terms with the King, but in 1783 he was glad to welcome as a guest at his Brighton establishment George III's 21 year old son and heir, George Prince of Wales, who liked the town so much he returned the following year and took a house on the Steyne. Enter Mrs Fitzherbert in 1785—she had a house of her own in the village of Litlington beside the Downs. The building of the first modest Pavilion with its balconies, low front and flattened cupola began in 1787. But the Prince had more flamboyant ideas, and ten years later he discussed them with the noted landscape designer Humphry Repton who in 1808 published a magnificent folio volume *Designs for the Pavilion at Brighton*. The outlandish eastern style of these with domes and minarets pleased Prinny immensely. It was Repton's partner John Nash, however, who obtained the building contract, and in 1817, as Christopher Marsden has written, 'brought the Prince's vision of an oriental pavilion to its astonishing fruition.' The locals called it Florizel's Folly.

THEATRE ROYAL, BRIGHTON.

Mr. LACY

Respectfully announces to his Friends and the Patrons of the Drama, that his

FAREWELL

BENEFIT

WILL TAKE PLACE

This Evening, THURSDAY,

SEPTEMBER 26, 1839,

Upon which occasion, although prevented by a lengthened and severe illness from becoming an active candidate for their favours, he trusts that he may be fortunate enough to obtain a renewal of the liberal support he has before experienced.

Mr. LACY is happy to inform his Patrons, that he has secured the services of that admirable Actress,

Mrs. HONEY,

Who will appear as KATE O'BRIEN, in PERFECTION.

The Performances will commence with the new Play, in Five Acts, called

RICHELIEU

OR, THE CONSPIRACY.

Written by Sir EDWARD LYTTON BULWER, Bart.

With entire New Scenery, Dresses, Armour, and Decorations.

Louis XIII.............................King of France,.......................Mr. WALLIS.	
Gaston.........................the Duke of Orleans, Brother of the King.............Mr. BURTON,	
Cardinal Richelieu, (Prime Minister)............	Mr. LACY.
The Chevalier Mauprat,.................Mr. GRAFTON.	
Count de Baradas, ...(favourite of the King, First Gentleman of the Chamber, &c.)............Mr. MULFORD.	
Count de Clermont ....Mr. COLWELL.	
The Sieur de Beringhen.........in attendance on the King, one of the Conspirators,.........Mr. C. HILL.	
Captain of Archers ...... Mr. FREDERICKS.	
Father Joseph.............a Capuchin, Richelieu's Confident,.........Mr. PHILLIPS.	
Huguet................Officer of Richelieu's Household Guard, a Spy,................Mr. SILVER.	
François, First Page to Richelieu,...............Mrs. C. HILL.	
Gaoler,.............Mr. ASBURY Governor of the Bastile.............Mr. BRADFORD.	

xxi

The atmosphere created by the Prince, an atmosphere divorced from any attempt of prophylaxis, part sporting, part theatrical, part military and always open-minded and open-handed, has clung to Brighton. . . . He left Brighton with a European reputation and some of the most charming as well as most extraordinary architecture in England.

For most it was the sea which attracted them to Brighton. It was declared not only safe but healthy—to drink as well! In 1786 a Dr Ainster published his *Thoughts on Brighthelmston Concerning Sea-Bathing and Drinking Sea-Water.* The beach was bracing. William Cobbett wrote that Brighton was thought by stock-jobbers to afford a salubrious air; great parcels of them stayed there with their women and children. 'They skip backward and forward on the coaches and actually carry on stock-jobbing in "Change Alley" though they reside in Brighton.' But in 1815 the local minister, Dr Styles, in a dread sermon warned against the temptations of watering places—'a state of idleness is perhaps more than any other incompatible with a state of salvation.'

The Duke of Clarence, who succeeded his brother George IV as William IV, knew Brighton well, and had a liking for the unique Chain Pier which had been erected in 1823. He showed it to Queen Adelaide shortly after his coronation. Queen Victoria paid an official visit to Brighton in 1837, the year of her succession; and another visitor in October that year was Charles Dickens who had finished all the instalments of *Pickwick Papers* and had started *Oliver Twist.* But he came to the resort to be idle and resisted the temptation to write. The Queen brought Prince Albert a few months after they were married in 1839, but they were ill at ease in the exotic Pavilion and never came to Brighton again. Frivolous Regency Brighton gave way to Respectable Victorian Osborne on the Isle of Wight. What did come to Brighton was the noisy, smelly train bringing noisy, rumbustious Cockneys to jostle the nobility and gentry on the esplanade.

Rich and Poor

On the day of Queen Victoria's coronation the keel was laid in the shipyard of Messrs Rickman and Godlee on the river Ouse at Lewes of the 120-ton *Lewes Castle,* the first ship ever built there. There were shipyards at this time too at Hastings, Littlehampton, Shoreham and Rye which was the start point of the shortest route across the English Channel to Boulogne 'by a fast and commodious sea-going steam vessel.' The return journey was often made to Brighton. Newhaven was not to be developed until some time later. These were the ports for traffic to the continent from all over England, mainly for business trips and holidays, but also for those going further afield, the host of emigrants who every week at the beginning of the nineteenth century were seeking a new life in the colonies. 'We learn from a correspondent in the eastern part of this county' ran an editorial in the *Brighton Gazette* in July 1839, 'that the desire to emigrate is becoming more frequent; the want of employment in the winter season inducing many to try their fortunes in another country. Upwards of forty persons of the labouring class departed from Lewes for London at four this morning to embark for South Australia' reported the *Sussex Advertiser* in January the same year. 'We have each £100 a year and live in a house—where could we do that in England?' wrote an Eastbourne emigrant to Australia.

Sussex was too large an area with too big a population (300,000) for a single local government unit to cope with, and the fair administration of Poor Relief for those who chose to slog it out at home suffered as a consequence. It was not until 1889 that separate West Sussex and East Sussex county councils were created to serve the three western rapes (from Chichester) and the three eastern rapes (from Lewes) respectively. It was still a single county with one Lord Lieutenant and one county town, the cathedral city of Chichester, for what was still 'Sussex'. Not until 1974 was the area divided into two *counties,* West Sussex and East Sussex, each with its capital and Lord Lieutenant.

For those who did not emigrate, life in mid-Victorian England was indeed tough—at the bottom. Well-disposed people at the top took measures to relieve the distress of the deserving poor but made few attempts to *cure* poverty. The Queen graciously gave twenty guineas to the Brighton Dorcas Charity 'towards the comfort of the poorer classes during the severity of the winter [of 1839].' Typical of a more sustained effort to bridge the gap between the Two Nations were the three well-endowed almshouses beneath the walls of the luxurious Petworth House. One for twelve poor men and women was built and endowed by a Mr Thompson; the Earl of Egremont's Almshouse gave shelter to four old people; Charles Duke of Somerset had founded one in the seventeenth century, a worthy charitable institution which two centuries later was still giving board and lodging to twenty-two widows.

Charles Seymour Duke of Somerset became the master of Petworth House when he married Lady Elizabeth Percy in 1670. Until then it had belonged to the powerful Percy Earls of Northumberland, who acquired it from King Henry I (1100–1135). The ninth Earl of Northumberland, known as the Wizard because of his interest in scientific experiments, added a long cellar in 1625. But his rebuilding ambitions were thwarted by having to spend the next sixteen years in the Tower of London for suspected complicity in the Gunpowder Plot. It was his great-granddaughter Lady Elizabeth Percy who between 1688 and 1693 transformed Petworth House and gave it the appearance it has today. The scale of restoration was inspired by her husband who, because of his obsession with his own nobility, was nicknamed The Proud Duke. Incorporated in the virtually new house was the chapel of the original castellated mansion of 1309.

The daughter of the Proud Duke of Somerset married Sir William Wyndham, and their son became the 2nd Earl of Egremont who succeeded to half the Seymour and Percy inheritance, including Petworth House. His son the 3rd Earl of Egremont was the patron of the landscape painter William Turner from whom he commissioned several pictures of Sussex all of which are hanging in the house today. Moreover he was a model employer, and allowed his farm workers to play bowls and cricket on his lawns, and even to write their names on his walls and windows. The artist Benjamin Haydon said the very flies at Petworth seemed to know there was room for their existence; 'dogs, horses, cows, deer and pigs peasantry and servants, guests and family, all shared in Lord Egremont's bounty and opulence.'

Rivalling the opulence of Petworth House was the magnificence of Goodwood House, the ancestral home of the Gordon Lennox family who became Dukes of Richmond. The first Duke of Richmond was the son of Merry Monarch Charles II and his mistress Louise de Querouaille. It was the fabulously wealthy Duke of Richmond who gave the famous ball in Brussels on the eve of the Battle of Waterloo—15 June 1815—attended by the Duke of Wellington and the principal officers of the British and Allied Army. It was something he never forgot, and at the dinner which he held at Goodwood every March for his tenants he always followed the toast to 'the Queen, may she long live over a moral and free people, and therefore a happy and contented nation' with a call for a bumper to the Great Hero of the Day, the Duke of Wellington and the Army. Dinner was served to the 200 guests at four in the afternoon and, as the local newspaper reported, 'the cloth was removed at 5.' The Duchess of Richmond, the Dowager Duchess and Lady Caroline Gordon Lennox (a bridesmaid at Queen Victoria's wedding) appeared in the orchestra balcony to listen to the speeches 'but it was not generally known that they were present.'

In 1801 the 3rd Duke of Richmond organised horse racing in the park of Goodwood House as a sport for the officers of the Sussex Militia of which he was colonel. The following year he established a proper private racecourse to which he admitted the public—the foundation of 'Glorious Goodwood' which began as a single annual meeting in July lasting four days and today consists of 15 meetings spread over May, July, August and September. In Victoria's reign it was one of the great social events of the year, with all the country mansions for miles around being let out for house parties at the inflated price of £100 a week or more. The dripping left over from the haunches of

Town Plan and View of Brighton by Richard Thomas, 1779

Until about the early nineteenth century Brighton was known as Brighthelmston and it was under this name it appeared on all early maps and engravings. This attractive town plan by a Brighton bookseller, Richard Thomas, sold for 2 shillings when it was printed in 1779. It has a key at he top pinpointing the taverns, schools, chapels and even 'The Bath' which must have been a very vital piece of information for visitors!

This plan was surveyed by Yeakell and Gardner who also made a very important map of Sussex which marked the start of a new era of scientific trigonometrical survey and was a forerunner of the early Ordnance Survey maps. Yeakell was a Dutch engraver but Gardner was probably a Sussex man. (By courtesy of the British Library)

REFERENCES to the HUNDREDS.

1	Dumford	21	Poynings	41	Alciston
2	Eastburne	22	Fishersgate	42	Flexborough
3	Westburne	23	Burbeech	43	Longbridge
4	Bosham	24	Tipnoake	44	Willingdon
5	Manhood	25	Windham	45	East Bourne
6	Box & Stockbridge	26	Dean	46	Dill
7	Liberty of Lodsworth	27	Preston	47	Pevensey Liberty
8	Rotherbridge	28	Whalesbone	48	Foxearle
9	Westeaswright	29	Youusmere	49	Hauxborough
10	Easteaswright	30	Hollingstrough	50	Loxfield Baker
11	Bury	31	Swanborough	51	Shoyswell
12	Avisford	32	Barcomb	52	Henhurst
13	Aldweek	33	Ringmer	53	Netherfield
14	Poling	34	Rushmonden	54	Nenfield
15	Brightford	35	East Grinstead	55	Bexhill
16	Stenning	36	Hartfield	56	Baldsloe
17	West Grinstead	37	Rotherfield	57	Battle
18	Shinglecrofs	38	Loxfield	58	Staple
19	Buttinghill	39	Shiplake	59	Goldspur
20	Street	40	Totnore	60	Gostrow 61 Guésli

A
MAP
of
SUSSEX,
from the best
AUTHORITIES.

Published by John Stockdale Piccadilly 28th March 1805.

Engraved by J. Cary.

Statute Miles 69½ to a Degree of Latitude

lamb and barons of beef roasted during Goodwood Week in their vast kitchens was on sale in the shops of Chichester for many a day after the guests had gone home to recover. The Silver Cup gave way to the Gold Cup in 1812, and then the Goodwood Cup, today one of the longest flat races in the calendar.

Of equal prominence was Arundel Castle—'Harundel' in Domesday Book—one of the three chief strongholds of Robert of Bellesme, son of Roger of Montgomery and Lord of West Sussex who took up arms against his king, Henry I, in 1101. Henry blockaded Arundel Castle and banished Robert after he had

surrendered, forfeiting the castle and all his Sussex land. Three of the six rapes of Sussex fell into the hands of the king who jealously kept Arundel for himself. He settled it in dower to his wife, Queen Adelais, who lived there after his death. Arundel and Pevensey were the only two places in Sussex which played any noticeable part in the civil war of Stephen's reign. The strong keep and formidable walls of Arundel Castle, then washed on one side by the sea, made it impregnable. Once more it was blockaded and forced to surrender. Stephen gave it to his son William, Count Mortain and Earl of Warenne. At that time the

---

Goodwood House

---

previous page

Sussex by John Cary, 1805

The greatest and most prolific of the nineteenth century mapmakers was John Cary (c 1754–1835) who steered away from the age of pretty and decorative maps to the more functional kind we know today. This map of Sussex gives an amazing amount of detail and each of the hundreds is circled in outline colour and numbered for identification. Clear up-to-date road classification is a feature of Cary's maps. It is interesting to note that Brighton is still called Brighthelmstone.

This is a second edition of Cary's map and was published by John Stockdale. It was originally sold separately and then issued in 1809 as part of the New English Atlas. *Cary was particularly interested in communication and he was commissioned by the Postmaster General to make a new survey of the mail coach routes and other roads. His work was recognised by the Royal Society who awarded him a medal in 1804. He has been described as 'the most representative, able and prolific of English cartographers' and many discerning map collectors have acquired examples of his work. (By courtesy of Cartographia, Southampton Street, London WC2)*

Sussex by Christopher and John Greenwood 1825

Early in the nineteenth century Christopher Greenwood conceived the ambitious plan of mapping all the English counties at the large scale of one inch to a mile. This section of Sussex is one of those. The whole map comes in six sections, which can be joined together, and kept in a slip case. Each map has a vignette, in this case, Chichester cathedral. The engraving is very detailed and gives an intricate picture of land-use as the enclosure movement was slowing down.

The publishing firm of C. & J. Greenwood flourished from about 1817 to 1834. Christopher and John were brothers who came from Gisburn in Yorkshire and their work was issued in direct competition with the Ordnance Survey, which gradually took over, and provides a great deal of detailed information of life in that period. (By courtesy of Ivan Deverall, Prints and Maps, Cambridge Way, Uckfield, Sussex)

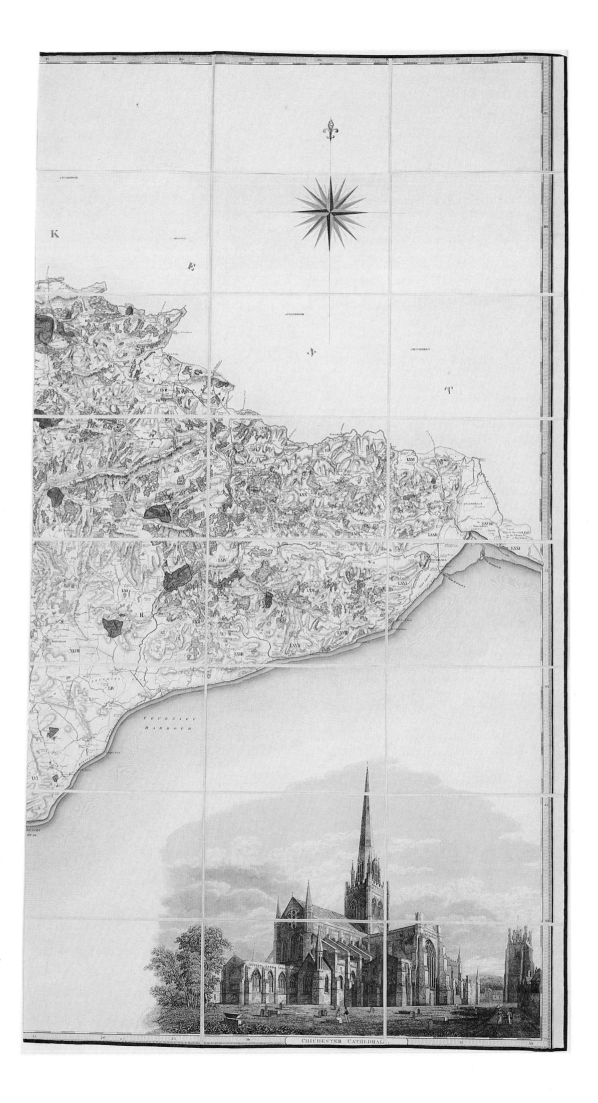

CHICHESTER CATHEDRAL.

Earl of Arundel was the greatest military tenant of Sussex, holding the Honour (Seignory) of Arundel under grant of Henry II and owing service of 84½ knights. Later it came into the hands of the Howard family who, as Dukes of Norfolk, were hereditary Earls Marshal of England. Henry VIII had a particular liking for Arundel, but when he paid it a ceremonial visit in 1526 it was already showing signs of decay. Between the end of the eighteenth century and the beginning of the twentieth, it was partially or wholly rebuilt three times, and little remains today of the medieval royal fortress. But it is still the property of the 16th Duke of Norfolk, though he no longer lives there.

Many other ancient families have lived generation to generation in fine mansions to be found all over Sussex, like the Shelleys of Lewes (the family of the poet who was born in the county in 1792); the Gages of Firle (Sir John Gage was Constable of the Tower of London to Henry VIII—the Greengage was named after them); the Brownes of Cowdray (Sir Anthony Brown was Master of the Horse to Henry VIII who gave him Battle Abbey after the Dissolution of the Monasteries). So many of the Norman barons who helped William conquer England never ventured further north than the county in which the decisive battle took place. Their descendants, with the corrupted French names which betray their lineage, lived in the houses they built on confiscated properties for centuries after. The family of John de Shoyswell (Choiseul) will have been living at Shoyswell Manor well before there is record of their doing so in 1377, and continued to live there through the reign of William III. The Courthope family are known to have been living in Wadhurst as early as 1295, but through marriage John Courthope came into the manor house of Whiligh in 1512, and George Courthope, the last male descendant (MP for Rye and made a baron in 1945) died there in 1955. Robert de Passele, Knight of the Shire of Sussex in 1296, lived in the still standing Pashley Manor, and the family had it as their home until 1452.

As Major General, Charles Lennox, the 4th Duke of Richmond became Colonel of the 35th Foot, or Earl of Donegall's, Regiment in 1803. Born in 1764 he fought a duel with the Duke of York in 1789. The 35th Foot Regiment had been raised in Belfast by order of King William III, and fifty-eight years later it was nicknamed 'The Orange Lilies' because of the orange facings of their uniforms denoting the Protestant origins. In 1804 the 35th Foot was re-named The Dorsetshire Regiment, and though it had no connection with that county (county titles encourage recruiting), it kept the name for the next 22 years. In 1826 it was re-named once again, The Sussex Regiment, and then in 1832 the orange regimental colour gave way to royal blue when William IV conferred the title of The Royal Sussex Regiment. They fought and died in both World Wars, and war memorials all over the county keep afresh the memory of their names and sacrifice. In 1966 it was amalgamated into The Queen's Regiment.

Sussex by Thomas Moule c. 1838

The county maps by Thomas Moule (fl. 1822–42) are eagerly sought-after by map collectors because they look so attractive framed and coloured. They usually contain local heraldry (which is not surprising as Moule was an heraldry expert) and the coats-of-arms on 'Sussex' are those of the See of Chichester, the Duke of Norfolk and the Earl of Egremont.

Moule's maps, which were first issued in parts and then appeared in his atlas entitled The English Counties Delineated *of 1942, were the last decorative series to be published.*

The insets show Arundel Castle, Chichester Cathedral and the famous chain pier at Brighton which was dramatically swept away in a gale during the winter of 1896. The pier, which had been opened in 1823 and been visited by Queen Victoria, was considered beautiful because of its simplicity of design. (By courtesy of Ivan Deverall, Uckfield, Sussex)

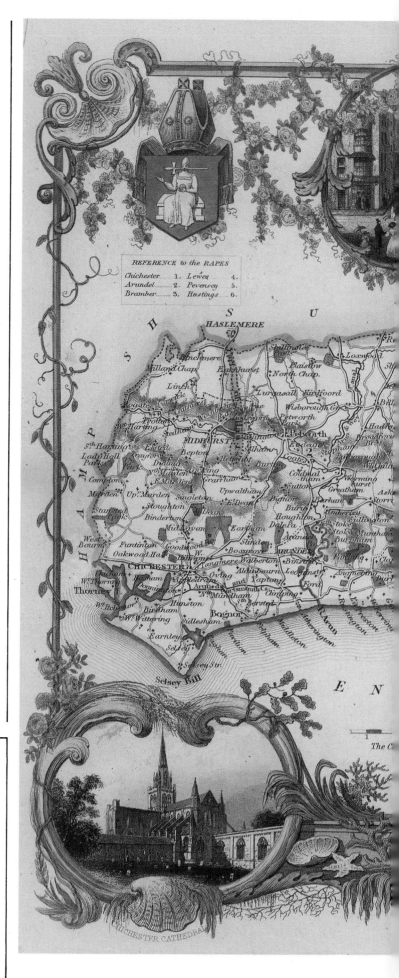

CHAIN PIER. BRIGHTON

CHICHESTER

SUSSEX

ARUNDEL CASTLE

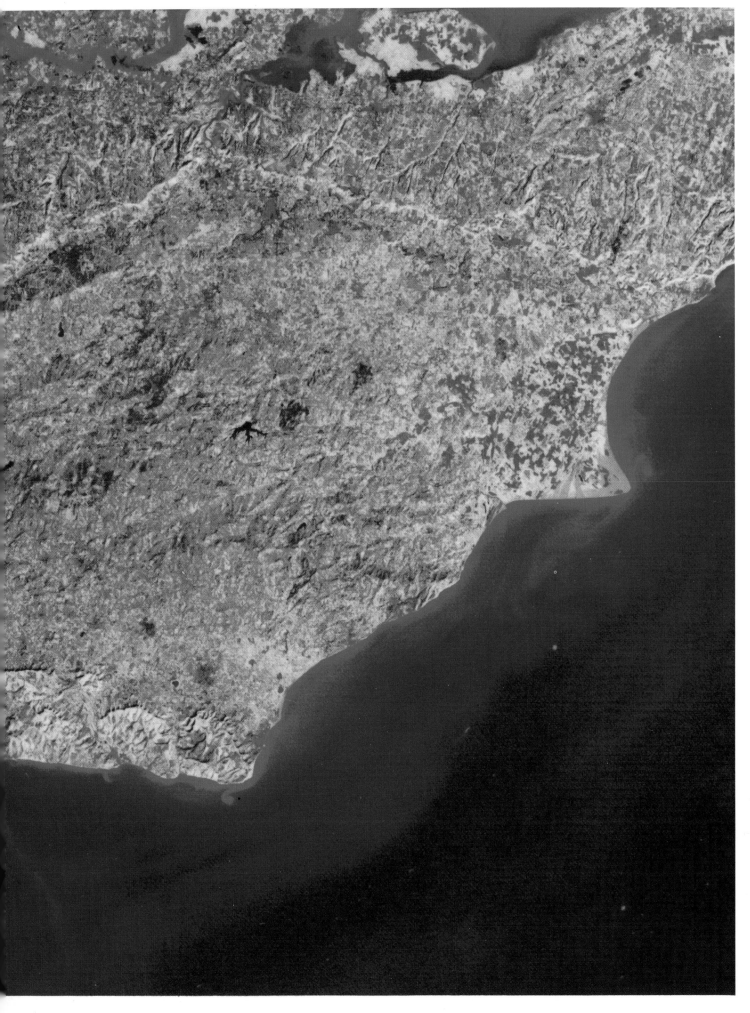

Landsat Satellite Image of Sussex

If the mapmakers of yesteryear were to return today and see all the modern aids for the surveyor, they would certainly be amazed. This photograph of Sussex, for example, was taken at an altitude of 920 kilometres (570 miles) above the earth from one of the first generation of three Landsat satellites which were remote sensing spacecraft orbiting the earth every 103 minutes. It was taken at 10.00 GMT on November 1979, and shows all the major features of the county in different colour bands.

Deep or clear water (sea, rivers, lakes and reservoirs) are shown in dark blue or black; shallow water, sediment laden water and estuaries are mid-light blue (coastal); haze, urban areas and bare fields are light blue (inland); woodland is red/brown; grassland and agricultural crops are red; natural grassland and heathland are in yellow/green; moorland or peat areas are green/brown, and cloud, snow, sandbanks and construction of roads and runways are shown in white.

This type of remote sensing measures solar-reflected energy in several bands of the spectrum and the reflection of this energy has different characteristics depending upon the surface's physical nature and structure. For instance, solid water and crops all have their own energy signature. This picture was prepared by combining band 4 (green part of the spectrum), band 5 (red) and band 7 (near infra-red) using blue, green and red filters respectively. The information it provides is not only useful to mapmakers but also to geologists, agriculturists, and in the study of pollution and oceanography.

The Martello Towers on the Sussex coast were re-commissioned in the Second World War to house more sophisticated weaponry to repel the latest invasion threat, but mercifully they never had to be fired. Large sections of the county were used to train the force that mounted the Allies' invasion of the enemy-occupied coast of France. Many mansions, golf clubhouses and halls were requisitioned as army headquarters, training schools and billets. The county had it share of bombs, flying and otherwise, and helped the defenders of London by shooting down so many enemy aircraft before they ever reached the barrage balloons which encircled the capital.

Charles Dawson, geologist, solicitor and steward of the manor of Barkham, dropped what he planned to be an archaeological bombshell in 1912 by claiming to have unearthed part of the skeleton of someone who had lived in Sussex some 250,000 or 500,000 years before—the Dawn Man who miraculously had survived the Ice Age. The site was Piltdown Common, but the

two wars had to be fought and won before Piltdown Man was exposed as a hoax. Dawson's 'discovery' was exploded and proved to be nothing more than a damp squib.

Sussex is essentially a peaceful county, with the aggressiveness of the Teddy Boys described by Graham Greene in *Brighton Rock* the exception. The fiercest contests are on the famous polo ground of Cowdray Park and the cricket pitch at Hove, home of the Sussex County Cricket Club which, formed in 1839, was England's first. As Prince of Wales in 1791 the future George IV presented Brighton with a cricket ground afterwards known as Ireland's Garden. His brother William IV subscribed £20 to the foundation of the Sussex County Cricket Club.

The spirit of Sussex is to be found in the evening supper parties in the garden of Christie's Glyndbourne opera house in the interval of impeccable performances of Monteverdi or Mozart, enjoying the performances of Britain's leading actors and actresses at the Chichester Festival, quaffing Lewes-brewed Harvey's bitter at Eastdean, backing the horses at Plumpton, picnicking in Ashdown Forest, sailing on Bewl Bridge Reservoir, sea surfing off Bexhill, hang gliding over Beachy Head, golfing at Dale Hill, envying the Long Man of Wilmington, admiring the topiary at Great Dixter, strolling across the wide open spaces of the South Downs with a high flying kite.

The forty year peace since 1945, if he had lived to see it, would have allowed Hilaire Belloc to fulfil the longing he made in his swinging verse *The South Country*:

> If I ever become a rich man
>   Or if I ever grow to be old,
> I will build a house with deep thatch
>   To shelter me from the cold.
> And there shall be Sussex songs to be sung
>   And the story of Sussex told.
> I will hold my house in the high wood
>   Within a walk of the sea,
> And the men that were boys when I was a boy
>   Shall sit and drink with me.

The dedication to the Lord Lieutenant of Sussex on Emanuel Bowen's map of the county published in mid-eighteenth century. The text underneath explains how the 'ancient town of Winchelsey was swallowed up by the Sea in a tempest Anno 1250, at which time the surface of the earth, both here and on the Kentish shoar, was much alter'd.' Left of the picture can be seen part of a plan of the new town. (By courtesy of Ivan Deverall, Maps and Prints, Cambridge Way, Uckfield, Sussex)

Famous Sussex Names

Ade
Albiney (de Albini)
Ashburnham
Baker
Bohun
Boorde
Breose (de Braose)
Browne
Bugsell
Burghersh
Burrell (Sir William)
Camoys
King Canute
Carver
Catt
Clulow
Cogger
Collins
Courthope
Covert
Crowhurst
Culpeper
St Cutham
Dalyngrigges
Darell
De Echyngham
De Hastings
De Herst (Monceaux)

De la Warr
De Shoyswell
De Warren
St Dunstan
Ellman
Elphinstone
King Ethelwulf
Fiennes (Baron Dacre)
Fitzalan (Earl of Arundel)
Fitzwalter
Fuller
Gage
Hessell
Hoo
Howard (Duke of Norfolk)
Hussey
Lennox (Duke of Richmond)
Le Despencer
Lewknor
Lower
Lumley
Maltravers
Mantell
Mascall
May
Montacute
Naylor
Neville (Earl of Abergavenny)

Newington
Otway
Oxenbridge
Pelham
Percy (Earl of Northumberland; Duke of N)
Petronilla
Radcliffe
Radmild
Roberts of Boarzell
Rowe
Sackville (Lord Buckhurst; Duke of Dorset)
Sayers
Seymour (Duke of Somerset)
Shelley
Shiffner
Shirley
Tattersall (Captain)
Turner
Vane (Fane)
Wardeux
Warenne (Earl and Countess de)
Webster
Windsor
Winterton
St Wilfrid (First Bishop of Sussex)
Wybarne
Wyndham (Earl of Egremont)

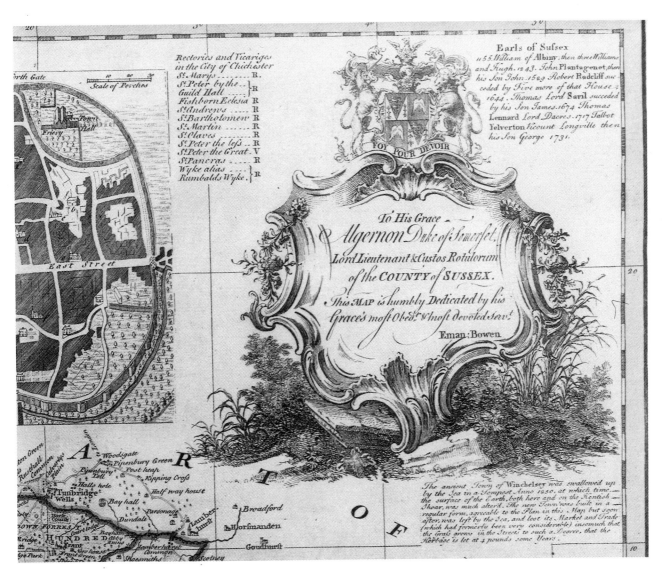

Bibliography

William Albery, *A Millenium of Facts in the History of Horsham and Sussex*, 1947.

Thomas Allen, *History of the Counties of Surrey and Sussex*, 2 vols, 1829–30.

Hugh Barty-King, *Sussex in 1839* (Osprey, The Landscape Histories, 1974).

John Booth, *Looking at Old Maps* (John Booth, Westbury, Wiltshire, 1979).

Henry Cheal, *The Story of Shoreham*, 1921.

Thomas Chubb, *The Printed Maps in the Atlases of Great Britain and Ireland 1579–1870* (Dawsons, London, Reprint, 1974).

William Cobbett, *Rural Rides*, 1830, George Woodcock ed. (Penguin English Library, 1967).

Gordon J. Copley (ed), Camden's *Britannia – Surrey and Sussex*, 1586, from the edition of 1789 by Richard Gough (Hutchinsons, 1977).

Daniel Defoe, *A Tour Through The Whole Island of Great Britain*, 1724–6, Pat Rogers ed. (Penguin English Library 1971).

Rev. Thomas Walker Horsfield, *History and Antiquities of Lewes*, 2 vols, 1824 *History, Antiquities and Topography of Sussex*, 2 vols, 1835.

Christopher Hussey, *A History of Scotney Castle*.

Gervase Jackson-Stops, *Petworth House Sussex*, An Illustrated Souvenir.

David Kingsley, *Printed Maps of Sussex 1575–1900* (Sussex Record Society, Volume 72, Lewes 1982), No. 110.

Local History Research Unit, East Sussex County Council, *Brighton in Tudor and Stuart Times* (ESCC, 1969).

Local History Research Unit, East Sussex County Council, *Gunfounding* (ESCC 1969).

M. A. Lower, *The Worthies of Sussex*, 1865 and *A Compendious History of Sussex*, 2 vols, 1870.

Christopher Marsden, *The English At The Seaside* (Collins, 1947).

Ester Meynell, *Sussex* (Robert Hale Ltd, London, 1949).

Carl Moreland and David Bannister, *Antique Maps* (Longman, London and New York, 1983).

William Page (ed), *The Victoria History of the Counties of England*, Sussex vols 1 & 2.

Pigot & Co's, *Royal National and Commercial Directory and Topography – Sussex*, 1839.

Recologea Papers, vol 9, no 1 (Robertsbridge Archaeological Society, Jan. 1982).

H. N. Shore, *Smuggling Days and Smuggling Ways*, 1892.

Ernest Straker, *Wealden Iron* (G. Bell, 1931).

Sussex County Magazine,, vol 22 (re Charles Dickens at Brighton).

R. V. Tooley, *Maps and Mapmakers*, (B. T. Batsford, London, 1970).

Coolie Verner, "Captain Collins' Coasting Pilot" in *Map Collectors Circle* (London, 1969).

Acknowledgements

My grateful thanks are due to John Freeman for some of the photography, to Linda Stacey for typing and to the following who loaned me maps: Bruce Marsden, Cartographia, Southampton Street, London WC2; Ivan Deverall, The Glen, Cambridge Way, Uckfield, Sussex; Anne Downs, Oldfield Maps and Prints, 34 Northam Road, Southampton; and Roger Baynton-Williams, Old Maps, Prints and Books, Maltravers House, Maltravers Street, Arundel, West Sussex.

Information about the authors

Valerie Scott is the editor of a quarterly journal called *The Map Collector* which is read by early map enthusiasts all over the world. She trained as a journalist and worked for newspapers and periodicals before starting *The Map Collector* in 1977. She is co-author of two earlier books in this series, *Buckinghamshire* and *Berkshire*. She lives with her three teenage children at Tring, Hertfordshire, and holds the International Map Collectors' Society award for being responsible for the 'cartographical contribution of greatest merit and widest interest to map collectors worldwide.'

Hugh Barty-King lives in Ticehurst on the East Sussex-Kent border. Educated at Winchester and Cambridge, he has been a full-time professional industrial and social historian since 1970, after many years in Government Information Services and Industrial Public Relations. His books include official histories of Cable and Wireless, the Automobile Association, the Baltic Exchange and the Guildhall School of Music and Drama; *Quilt Winders and Pod Shavers*, the story of the English Cricket Ball and Bat makers; *A Tradition of English Wine*; *Rum Yesterday and Today* (with Anton Massel); *New Flame*, a social history of Gas; *Expanding Northampton* and *Sussex in 1839*. His *Scratch A Surveyor . . .* tells the 250-year-old story of surveyors and valuers Drivers Jonas, 1725–1975.

ST. JOHN SMITH

Chartered Surveyors - Estate Agents - Auctioneers - Valuers

On 15th July 1879 George St. John Smith began his career as an agricultural valuer and auctioneer in one room at 196 High Street, Uckfield.

Today, St. John Smith, spanning Sussex with 6 offices from Brighton to Tunbridge Wells, are still controlled from the fine Georgian building at Uckfield.

They have achieved a reputation as specialists in the sale of country properties, based on the expertise of four generations of a family practice and on a thoroughly professional approach allied to modern methods of marketing. But as Chartered Surveyors they offer a lot more, from building design, surveying and planning services to the valuation and sale of commercial property, farms and furniture.

St. John Smith are delighted to be associated with this book about the County in which they are so fortunate to practise.